Home Office Research Study 216

Risk of Re-offending and Needs Assessments: the user's perspective

Natalie Aye Maung and Nicola Hammond

Home Office Research Studies

The Home Office Research Studies are reports on research undertaken by or on behalf of the Home Office. They cover the range of subjects for which the Home Secretary has responsibility. Titles in the series are listed at the back of this report (copies are available from the address on the back cover). Other publications produced by the Research, Development and Statistics Directorate include Research Findings, the Research Bulletin, Statistical Bulletins and Statistical Papers.

The Research, Development and Statistics Directorate

RDS is part of the Home Office. The Home Office's purpose is to build a safe, just and tolerant society in which the rights and responsibilities of individuals, families and communities are properly balanced and the protection and security of the public are maintained.

RDS is also a part of the Government Statistical Service (GSS). One of the GSS aims is to inform Parliament and the citizen about the state of the nation and provide a window on the work and performance of government, allowing the impact of government policies and actions to be assessed.

Therefore -

Research Development and Statistics Directorate exists to improve policy making, decision taking and practice in support of the Home Office purpose and aims, to provide the public and Parliament with information necessary for informed debate and to publish information for future use.

"The views expressed in this report are those of the authors, not necessarily those of the Home Office (nor do they reflect Government policy)."

First published 2000
Application for reproduction should be made to the Communications and Development Unit, Room 201, Home Office, 50 Queen Anne's Gate, London SW1H 9AT.

© Crown copyright 2000   ISBN 1 84082 571 5
                         ISSN 0072 6435

Foreword

It has been recognised for some time that there is a need for a standardised assessment instrument to inform prison and probation staff of the needs of offenders and their risk of re-offending. In order to develop such an instrument, the strengths and weaknesses of existing assessment instruments should be identified. This report summarises a study commissioned by the Home Office to examine the users perspective of assessment instruments currently in use in probation services in England and Wales. The study was designed to inform the development of a national joint prison-probation service assessment instrument. It concentrates on two assessment instruments, the ACE and LSI-R, and adapted versions of these tools.

Probation staff who had experience of the instruments were interviewed. The focus of the interviews was to examine the extent of the use of the assessment instruments and what were the perceived strengths and weaknesses of the tools. The study concludes that assessment tools were widely used and performed a variety of functions, including assisting in the production of PSRs and completing supervision plans. Overall, the use of a standardised assessment tool was seen as being useful in assisting the work of probation staff. The report also summarises particular benefits and limitations of the individual instruments, and makes certain recommendations for the development and implementation of a national assessment instrument.

Chris Lewis
Head of Offenders and Corrections Unit
Research Development and Statistics Directorate

Acknowledgements

We would like to thank all the officers who we interviewed in the study, who were extremely generous with their time and open about their experiences. We would also like to acknowledge the help of Andrew Bridges (Berkshire), Mike Maiden (Durham), Gill Roberts and Claudia Lewis-Moore (Hereford and Worcestershire), Christine Lawrie and Mark Oldfield (Kent), Peter Sugden (Teeside) and Brian Langley (Northumbria), James Gritton (Surrey), David Gardiner (Northumbria), Diana Fulbrook (Warwickshire), Janet Chaplin (West Glamorgan) and Liz Stafford (West Midlands) in allowing us access to officers, assisting us greatly in the interviewing stages and in providing information themselves about the experiences in their services.

Colin Roberts provided useful background about the ACE project and Peter Davies of the CCF gave us information about services using LSI-R. We would also like to thank Carol Hedderman for her help at all stages of this research.

NATALIE AYE MAUNG
NICOLA HAMMOND

Contents

Summary

Background and methodology

- The Home Office is shortly to pilot a new national risk and needs assessment system for all probation services and the Prison Service. A small-scale study was carried out in order to inform the specification for the new instrument. The main aim of this study was to look at the practical experiences and attitudes of officers using risk and needs assessment tools, particularly ACE and LSI-R. Two other locally developed tools for assessment of risk and needs, the Kent CMI and Berkshire AF were also examined.

- Researchers interviewed 21 senior probation officers (SPOs) and 50 probation officers (POs), including 18 ACE and 22 LSI-R users, in ten probation service areas. Three services used ACE, four used LSI-R, one had just completed an evaluation of both, and the remaining two – Kent and Berkshire – used locally developed instruments.

- LSI-R is a two-page form, consisting of a list of 54 factors related to re-offending. Officers score each factor, which are added up to obtain the "Total LSI-R score" for the offender. There is a small space for notes and a professional discretion over-ride section.

- ACE is a series of separate forms, consisting of an initial assessment form, a supervision plan, a quarterly progress form, and a self-completion form for offenders. The ACE forms vary slightly between different services implementing them, although there are core elements common to all services. The initial assessment covers both criminogenic and non-criminogenic needs, and includes some details about risk of harm.

- CMI is a stand-alone form, which is started at the pre sentence report (PSR) stage and for all new commencements, and completed on an ongoing basis throughout the order. The form has two main components: a risk assessment profile, which includes a dangerousness/risk of harm checklist; and a case management plan which lists 18 potential needs or factors. The case management plan is reviewed every three months.

- The AF is very different to the other instruments. It does not directly seek to structure the assessment, but asks officers to specify which outcomes they will target in order to reduce the likelihood of offending. The stand-alone form comprises three components: compliance with National Standards; reducing the Likelihood of Offending (where outcomes are specified); managing the risk of dangerousness behaviour. Needs are re-assessed every three months.

Main purpose(s) of the instruments

- About a third of the 22 LSI-R users saw it as a dual assessment tool for risks and needs. Just under half the officers thought it was a risk assessment tool only.

- Over half the 18 officers using ACE said its main purpose was to help them in some way with assessments. A third said it was to help them look at progress and evaluate how effective their practice was, and four thought it informed their decisions about what to do with offenders.

- Four out of the five officers using the CMI saw it as assisting in risk assessment, and three as improving case management.

- Four of the five officers using the AF said it gave structure to their work.

Use of ACE, LSI-R and CMI

(i)   At the PSR stage

- All of the CMI users, nearly all the officers using LSI-R and over two-thirds of the ACE users completed assessments using the instruments at the PSR stage. A third of ACE users also employed the self-completion questionnaire at the PSR stage.

- All of the CMI and most of the ACE users said the instrument they used contributed to the PSR, for example, by keeping the officer focused or making assessments more thorough. Ten ACE users and all the CMI officers said the instruments were useful at this stage.

- Half the LSI-R users said that LSI-R did not help them write the PSR at all. Eight officers said it could contribute as a means of focusing on certain areas, acting as a checklist or structuring the interview.

(ii) At the start of supervision and input to supervision planning

- The main use of ACE at the start of supervision was in completing the supervision plan. Over two-thirds of users said that initial assessment informed the supervision plan, by improving objectives and highlighting problems to be addressed. Two officers said ACE did not help them write the supervision plan.

- Most CMI users said it contributed to the supervision plan.

- Just over a third of LSI-R users said their instrument fed into supervision planning. However, the same number said it did not, mainly because it was superceded by the PSR or supervision plan itself.

- In three of the services covered, the final LSI-R score was used to determine the level of supervision that offenders received.

(iii) During the order

- The CMI includes a quarterly review of needs/problems, although most officers interviewed did not have much experience of using this.

- ACE users carried out quarterly reviews as well as re-assessments of offender at the six or nine-month point. Five-sixths of those interviewed had used the quarterly progress forms; 10 said they had been involved in re-assessments.

- Half the ACE users who had done re-assessments found it helpful, e.g. in reviewing what had been done, or modifying objectives. However, the same number found it limited, because of the small change observed, problems with paperwork and the fact ACE did not add very much to what they would do anyway.

- Only seven LSI-R users had carried out re-assessments using the form, mainly because re-assessments were not done in their local service or because few orders had yet the relevant point for assessment. Half of these officers had used it to highlight or check areas of improvement, whereas the other half felt it was of limited use in measuring an offender's progress.

(iv) At the end of order

- There was little information available on how instruments were used at the end of the order.

(v) Carrying out the actual assessment

- About three-quarters of the LSI-R users filled the form in after an assessment interview, having covered the relevant topics with the offenders previously. The remaining quarter of officers tended to use the form with the offender during the interview itself. Four officers said they did not use the form either as a guide or a questionnaire, implying it was peripheral to their assessments.

- About two-thirds of the officers said offenders were not involved in completing the forms at all. When offenders were involved in completing the forms, reactions were either positive or neutral.

- Use of the initial ACE assessment form was varied, depending on the capability and interest of the offender, how well the officer knew them and how accustomed they were to probation. About a third of ACE users said they normally gathered information for the ACE assessment during an initial interview and filled out the forms afterwards. The same number went through part or all of the form during the interview.

- All of the CMI officers used the form as a guide to what they talked about with offenders in interviews. Four officers actively referred to the forms during interviews as appropriate and one tended to complete the form after they had done the interview.

(vi)   *Administering the ACE self-completion questionnaire*

- About half the officers who used the self-completion form let offenders complete it by themselves. The same number had variable practice, either filling in the form with offenders or letting them do it by themselves. Seven officers used this form to initiate discussions with the offender. Six officers reported difficulties with the form if the offender had problems reading or writing.

Use of the AF (outcomes required to reduce the likelihood of re-offending)

- Two out of the five officers interviewed completed this part of the AF at the PSR stage; the others did it at the start of supervision.

- In two cases it was unclear whether the AF had any direct impact on the assessment itself. However, three of the officers seemed to be using the list of outcomes as a means of structuring or at least checking their assessments.

- Four of the officers said that offenders were aware of the form as it was being completed, but only two officers said they directly involved offenders in completing the form.

- Three of the officers said the AF contributed to supervision planning, by focussing the direction of supervision and in forming the supervision plan itself.

- Three officers found it useful in measuring offenders' progress, while two did not. Officers found it useful in reviewing the order and modifying outcomes and in engaging the offender with progress. However, three officers said that the form often did not reflect progress made.

- Most officers using LSI-R, ACE and CMI felt that the PSR stage was one of the best times to complete an assessment and that some form of re-assessment should be done during supervision. (This question was not asked of AF users.)

- About a third of LSI-R-using officers said they usually or sometimes disagreed with other officers' assessments, compared to only two out of 18 ACE-using officers, no CMI users and two AF users. The most common reason that LSI-R users gave for disagreement was that offenders had disclosed more to the officer since the first assessment.

- At least half the officers in each group felt that there was overlap between information needed for the instruments and other forms, mainly with risk of harm paperwork and the repetition of standard offence and demographic information. The problem was worst in Kent, where the pilot had only just been completed and some forms were being duplicated.

- Only four ACE users had access to computerised versions of the instruments.

Training

- Most of the officers using ACE and LSI-R had at least a day's training to use the instruments. However, two officers who had recently started using ACE had not received any formal training, although both would have liked some.

- There was no formal training for the Kent and Berkshire instruments, but most users were broadly content with this.

- Most officers using ACE, CMI and AF were content with the length of their training.

- Nearly half the officers using LSI-R said the content of their training was not suitable. The main complaints were about the use of the video, the fact it did not address officers' queries or concerns, that it was too slow and too 'Canadian'.

Strengths

- Most of the LSI-R, ACE and CMI users said that the tool they used helped assessments in some way, particularly in acting as a check-list for the assessment, keeping them focused on relevant areas for assessment and giving structure to the interview (apart from CMI). ACE users also said that the forms helped them to ask difficult questions.

- ACE, LSI-R and CMI were also seen by most users as having a role in supervision planning. LSI-R and CMI users said they helped by focusing on issues that needed to be addressed. The main benefit of ACE here was that it helped in writing the supervision plan.

- Over two-thirds of the ACE-using officers thought it was useful for working directly with offenders, to raise issues or problems or initiate discussion with them.

- Half the LSI-R users saw it as a more objective, scientific process, which provided credibility to officers' assessments.

- About a third of the ACE users and most of the AF and CMI officers said the instruments impacted on the supervision process itself, mainly in demonstrating offenders' progress on an order (apart from AF) and in providing a structure for supervision. Two CMI users also mentioned its use in case management.

- About a third of officers using LSI-R and ACE and three using AF said the instruments provided information about a case, LSI-R and AF as a summary and ACE giving a fuller picture of a case.

- Six officers saw LSI-R as being useful for management, especially in allocating and targeting resources.

- One of the main benefits of the AF was that it made the assessment quicker, mainly because there was less paperwork and administration to complete.

Weaknesses

- Eighteen officers using LSI-R and 13 using ACE had problems filling in existing questions on the form. The most common problems were unclear wording of items (both), Americanised language (LSI-R), use of double negatives (LSI-R), reliance on offender information (LSI-R) and subjectivity of forms (ACE). Four CMI users cited a problem in the form in assessing offenders' motivation.

- The most common complaint among ACE users (17/22) was that the forms were burdensome to complete in some way: taking too much time, adding to paperwork, being repetitious, not fitting in with computing systems and the quarterly progress forms being required too frequently. Just under half the LSI-R interviewees and 2 of the CMI officers said that the forms were a burden to complete.

- About three-quarters of the LSI-R officers felt it did not contribute to their work, either because it did not tell them anything that they did not already know or that it did not feed into current systems. About a third of the ACE users felt this way.

- Fifteen officers using LSI-R felt that it missed out or lacked detail in certain areas, particularly risk of harm.

- Most of the AF and CMI users, and about two-thirds of the officers using LSI-R and ACE had concerns about limitations of the forms. Four AF users felt that the forms were too condensed, and they were not transparent to offenders or other officers, for example, in the case of transfer. LSI-R users wanted more space for officers' opinions. Users of LSI-R, ACE and CMI felt that the forms did not portray individuals accurately. ACE users also thought that such forms were not appropriate for their work or were not transparent to other parties.

- Half the officers using LSI-R expressed concerns about the inclusion of certain items in the form, mainly because they thought items were not relevant to re-offending or that there were too many static factors.

Usefulness in different aspects of work

- The majority of officers rated ACE and LSI-R as useful in terms of prioritising problems to be addressed. However, the performance of ACE/OGRS in measuring the risk of re-offending was not so good. None of the instruments performed particularly well on case recording.

Using the forms in middle management

- Most of the SPOs interviewed did not use, or had fairly short experience of using, the instruments for management purposes.

- LSI-R was seen as having potential in allocation and targeting of resources, getting summary information on team caseloads, supervising officers' work, and demonstrating effectiveness and progress. Few officers actually used LSI-R for these functions.

- ACE was seen as being potentially helpful in supervising officers' work (monitoring work done and checking referrals), providing information and allocating cases. Its role in actually monitoring assessments was seen as limited.

- One problem in using ACE and LSI-R for management purposes lay in ensuring that the forms were being filled out correctly and consistently.

- At the time of the pilot, the AF was being used to monitor officers' work (use of resources, referrals, enforcement) and to allocate cases. The concise nature of the form made it a useful summary of cases, but also put limitations on how much it could be relied on to give a full picture.

- CMI was not yet being used fully for management purposes, but it was seen as having a role in monitoring officers' work (supervision activities, referrals, use of time and resources) and in helping to target the Kent reporting scheme.

- Most managers rated ACE and LSI-R as useful (or potentially useful) in ensuring consistency in assessments, monitoring the quality of assessments and supervision, managing caseloads and in providing management information. AF was seen as useful in ensuring consistency of assessments, but not for monitoring their quality.

Suitability for all groups

- About three-quarters of the LSI-R users and about half the ACE officers said that the instruments were not suitable for all types of offenders, in particular sex offenders (both), juveniles (LSI-R), motoring offenders (both), domestic violence (LSI-R), trivial offenders (ACE), women (both), lifers (ACE) and older people (LSI-R). Only one officer each using AF and CMI felt they were unsuitable for all groups.

Supplementary tools in use

- Very few officers used additional tools to ACE, LSI-R or the locally developed instruments. The most commonly mentioned was OGRS. Eleven officers had some scepticism about OGRS' performance, the main complaint being that it gave questionable results for individual offenders, while seven officers thought it was useful in some way.

Links with prison assessments

- Some officers also commented about the links between probation and prison risk assessments and thought that the present situation could be improved by making assessment procedures consistent between prisons and probation.

- Officers currently experienced problems due to inconsistencies between prison and probation risk assessment procedures, duplication between the procedures, inconsistency within the prison system and general pressures on dealing with throughcare cases.

- A few officers had found the instruments useful in dealing with offenders on throughcare.

Assessing risk of harm and dangerousness

- The LSI-R form does not cover risk of harm at all; all services had concurrent procedures to assess this. Half the officers using LSI-R saw this as a limitation of the instrument. Five POs wanted forms to include both risk of re-offending and harm, and four officers thought that certain questions on LSI-R could be expanded to cover harm.

- The ACE assessment includes a short section on risk of harm and dangerousness, although some services had additional procedures to assess and manage this. Half the officers thought the ACE assessment was useful, while half did not.

- Advantages of the ACE risk of harm questions were seen as helping to focus the officers' thinking, making them more thorough and giving a more standard definition of risk of harm (two responses each). However, two officers showed some confusion about the role of the risk of harm assessment.

- In terms of limitations, four officers felt ACE was too basic and unspecific, and two that it was inappropriate to administer to all offenders.

- The Kent CMI incorporates the risk of harm assessment for the service.

- Four of the five officers interviewed found the structure of the different factors helpful in assessing risk of harm and dangerous offenders, in making them focus and be more thorough, and two said it had been useful in clarifying the distinction between risk of harm and re-offending.

- The Berkshire AF includes management of risk of harm, although other tools are also used.

- Officers completed additional forms to the AF on potentially dangerous offenders (PDOs) and this alleviated the most common criticism of the AF - that it did not allow officers to record enough information about the offender.

- Two officers said it made harm assessments more concise and specific.

Recommendations

- The study makes a number of recommendations for the implementation of any new national structured assessment:

- The new assessment procedure should be based on the "system" approach, linked into existing probation supervision procedures. The "system" should comprise, at minimum, an initial assessment, the supervision plan and review forms for progress.

- An initial assessment should be carried out at the PSR stage, for all offenders going on to community supervision or custody.

- Officers' use of the existing assessments gave clear lessons for the design of the forms, inclusion of particular items and wording used for individual items.

- In assessment, officers should be encouraged to use the forms as topic guides, rather than questionnaires, and treat the offender as the main, but not only, source of information.

- There is scope for including forms, or elements of forms, which can be used in work with offenders directly.

- The assessment system could play an active role in measuring and demonstrating progress to officers, offenders and other interested parties, although reviews should not be over-frequent.

- Construction of a structure for making explicit links between levels of assessed risk of re-offending and levels of supervision should be explored in the new system.

- The feasibility of making the initial assessment act as a trigger for referrals and other assessments should be examined.

- The scope for including risk of harm needs to be examined further. Possible models for incorporation exist.

- There is definite scope for the instrument to feed into case management, including provision of information on work done and resources used.

- The system should aim to be a case record for the officer, and therefore must be designed to adequately record progress.

- The introduction of the new assessment system should be linked as closely as possible to CRAMS and/or computerisation, and align with existing systems as far as possible. The assessment system itself should keep form-filling to the minimum required.

- Moves to bring prison and probation systems closer together would generally be welcomed, although this applies to risk of harm assessment as well as risk of re-offending.

- Some thought could be given to the merits of allowing a degree of flexibility to local services within the national assessment structure.

There were also some lessons to be learned about training for any new system:

- In some services, there had been initial resistance to the new instruments, for a variety of reasons.

- Training should not be seen separately from ongoing evaluation and development of the new system. It is important that there is an active practitioner input into the development of the form.

- The initial training should clearly explain the purpose of the instrument, and briefly describe the underlying theories.

- It should clearly justify the inclusion of each item, or in certain cases, the omission of certain items.

- The training should be hands-on, with plenty of examples and practical exercises and directly relevant to probation work.

- It should set out the best way to administer the instruments, using the forms as a guide to discussion and using all available sources of information.

- The potential benefits of the instruments should be made clear, but the limitations of the instrument should also be discussed. It should also recognise the different impact of the instruments on older and newer officers.

- The training must focus on and answer officers' queries and concerns and allow for some feedback on the system. One way in which this was done was to split the training to allow officers to use the instrument in practice and then come back to more training.

- The training for any new assessment system should link in with What Works training and other initiatives.

- Training on the new instrument must be part of any ongoing induction programme to ensure all officers are trained in the new system.

Chapter 1 Introduction

Background

The Home Office is shortly to pilot a new national risk and needs assessment system for all probation service areas and the Prison Service. In order to inform the specification for the new instrument, a small-scale study was carried out, looking at the practical experiences and attitudes of officers using risk and needs assessment tools.

The search for a more formal assessment tool for use by probation services derives in part from efforts to improve the way that services assess risk of re-offending. An HMIP inspection (HMI, 1995) and a Home Office research report by Burnett (1996) found that services were not performing this function well. A variety of steps were taken in response to these findings, including the development of the Offending Group Reconviction Scale or OGRS (Copas, 1998), an actuarial scale used to predict the risk of reconviction within two years; and research by Aubrey and Hough (1997) to look at the benefits of using different types of assessment scales. A number of services also developed or adopted structured assessment tools to determine risk and needs of offenders. The use of such tools has also been encouraged by other initiatives such as the What Works project and moves towards Effective Practice (see, for example, Chapman and Hough, 1998).

Up to now, the two most commonly used assessment scales in probation areas have been LSI-R (Level of Service Inventory - Revised), originally developed in Canada, and ACE (Assessment, Case recording and Evaluation), which has been developed by the University of Oxford working with Warwickshire Probation Service. The current research therefore focuses on ACE and LSI-R, but also covers the use of two locally developed instruments from Kent and Berkshire. The Kent instrument was included as this was promoted by that service as a workable alternative to ACE and LSI-R. The Berkshire Assessment Framework provides a very different approach to assessment to the previous three tools. This study complements the work being carried out by Raynor and Roberts, which makes a statistical comparison between the two most commonly used assessment scales, ACE and LSI-R.

The main aims of this research are:

a)   to describe the experiences of officers using ACE, LSI-R and locally developed instruments, in particular:

- how they use the instrument to assess and manage risk, and plan supervision;

- what they find useful about each instrument;

- what they find problematic or unnecessary;

- what is lacking or inadequately covered in each instrument;

b) to find out whether supplementary risk/needs assessment tools are used and if so, what these add to ACE or LSI-R;

c) to examine the suitability of ACE and LSI-R for special groups of offenders (women, mentally disordered offenders, substance abusers, sexual offenders, juvenile offenders) and suggest alternative methods and approaches for the accurate assessment of their risk and needs.

Methodology

Researchers visited ten Probation Service areas:

- three areas using ACE: Warwickshire, Hereford and Worcester, and West Midlands;

- four areas using LSI-R: West Glamorgan, Surrey, Durham and Teeside;

- one area which had just completed an evaluation of both ACE and LSI-R: Northumbria;

- two areas using alternative tools: Berkshire and Kent.

The areas were chosen to provide a range of those using ACE and LSI-R, including services where the use of the instrument was well established and others which had only recently started using these instruments (see Table 1.3 below).

In each area, face-to-face interviews were carried out with five probation officers (POs) with experience of using the instruments and two middle managers (senior probation officers or senior practice managers) who had direct experience of managing staff who were using these instruments. The interview schedule for POs focused on their use of the assessment instrument, any benefits and problems they found and their general attitudes towards using it. The interview schedule for middle managers was concerned with how they used the instrument in managing staff. In all, 21 senior probation officers (SPOs) or their equivalent, and 50 POs were interviewed by researchers, following an interview schedule (a list of the questions on this schedule is given in Appendix A). Senior managers or research staff were also interviewed in each area, in order to give background and context to the introduction and implementation of the instruments in each area. However, the focus of this report is on probation officers' and middle managers' use of the instruments and their perceptions of them.

Description of the samples

The PO sample contained a wide range of officers in terms of length of service (Table 1.1). The average length of service for POs in the ACE sample was 10.1 years, in the LSI-R sample 9.0 years and in the local sample 9.5 years. SPOs tended to be longer serving: the average length of service was 14.0 years for the ACE sample, 14.5 years for the LSI-R sample and 17.5 years for the local sample.

Table 1.1 Length of service: PO sample

	ACE	LSI-R	Kent	Berkshire
Length of service:				
2 years or less	3	3	2	1
Over 2 but less than 5 years	4	6	1	0
Over 5 but less than 10 years	4	6	0	2
10 years or more	7	7	2	2
Mean length of service (years)	10.1	9.0	7.6	11.3
Total in sample	18	22	5	5

Officers were asked what their current duties were (Table 1.2). Five out of six POs in the ACE sample (15 out of 18) and all POs in the Kent and Berkshire samples could be characterised as doing "generic" work i.e. they were involved in writing PSRs and supervising orders (and licenses). By contrast, just over half (13 out of 22) of the LSI-R sample did "generic" work, while six of them worked in specialist court teams, only writing PSRs and performing court duty.

Reflecting the differences between POs, most (6) SPOs in the ACE sample and all the SPOs in the Kent and Berkshire samples managed generic teams. Only two SPOs in the LSI-R sample managed generic teams.

Table 1.2 Type of work: PO sample

	ACE	LSI-R	Kent	Berkshire
Type of work:				
"Generic":				
Writing PSRs, supervising orders and licenses	9	1	4	2
Writing PSRs, supervising orders	6	11	1	2
Writing PSRs, supervising programmes	0	1	0	1
Specialist:				
Supervising orders only	0	1	0	0
Dedicated court teams	1	6	0	0
Dedicated throughcare teams	2	2	0	0
Total in sample	18	22	5	5

Notes:
a. Generic officers could also have been involved in supervising offenders on programmes. Some officers wrote only a small amount of PSRs on existing clients.
b. Officers in throughcare teams were sometimes involved in writing PSRs on existing clients, but this tended to be a very small part of their workload.

One factor which might affect officers' use and views of any instrument is the length of time they have been using it. More experienced users might be more favourable towards it as they have got used to it, while newer users may still be experiencing teething troubles. Length of use also reflects how long an instrument has been available in the local service, and there may be differences, for example, in how integrated an instrument is with other service procedures and administration. Each of the samples contained a range of newer and older users (Table 1.3). However, users of ACE and in Berkshire tended to be longer-term users. All but two of the ACE sample, and all of the AF users had been working with the instruments for over six months. By contrast, only half the LSI-R users had been using it for that long, while all of the officers in Kent had been using the CMI for less than a year.

Table 1.3 Length of use of instrument: PO sample

	ACE	LSI-R	Kent	Berkshire
Length of use:				
6 months or less	2	11	1	0
Over 6 months up to 12 months	6	6	4	1
12 months and over	10	5	0	4
Mean length of use (in months)	13.0	8.9	6.6	13.0
Total in sample	18	22	5	5

SPOs were also asked how long their team had been using the instrument. Reflecting the table above, 5 out of 8 in the ACE sample said their team had been using the instrument for over 12 months. Both Berkshire SPOs managed teams which had been using the AF for over a year. By contrast, only 3 out of the 9 SPOs in the LSI-R sample managed teams who had been using LSI-R for over a year. Both the Kent teams surveyed had been using the CMI for less than a year.

All the POs interviewed except for one of the ACE users were currently using the instrument in their work. Two SPOs out of nine in the ACE sample also used ACE currently to make assessments, and two others had done in the past. Similarly, two SPOs in the LSI-R sample currently used it to make assessments and one SPO was a past user. None of the SPOs in Kent or Berkshire had ever been regular users of the instruments.

The main four instruments examined

This section gives a brief description of the four instruments examined in the study: LSI-R, ACE, the Kent CMI and the Berkshire AF.

(i)   LSI-R

LSI-R is a two-page form, consisting of a list of 54 factors grouped into the following headings: criminal history, education/employment, financial, family/marital, accommodation, leisure/recreation, companions, alcohol/drug problem, emotional/personal and attitudes/orientation. (A copy of the LSI-R form is included in Appendix B.) Officers score individual factors either as yes/no items or on a scale from 3 to 0, according to how "satisfactory" the situation is and how much "improvement" is needed. Officers make a cross over the appropriate response for each question: these then transfer through to the back sheet, where they are added up to obtain the "Total LSI-R score" for the offender. There is a small space for notes and a professional discretion over-ride section, which officers may complete. A manual is also available providing fuller detail and guidance.

(ii)   ACE

ACE, by contrast, is a system-a series of separate forms. The ACE forms vary between different services implementing them, although there are core elements common to all services. A version of the forms is included in Appendix C, although services implementing ACE will usually customise these locally, for example, adding extra items or adapting the cover to fit in with local administration systems. The main (though not all) variations are noted below. Very broadly, the main forms are:

- an initial assessment form completed by POs. This covers both criminogenic and non-criminogenic needs, grouped broadly into social factors (e.g. accommodation, finances), personal factors (e.g. substance abuse, health) and offending (e.g. lifestyle, attitudes). The latter includes some details about risk of harm. All services using ACE apart from West Midlands carried out this initial assessment at PSR stage. POs in the West Midlands carried it out at the start of supervision. The form also includes an "assessment wheel" which visually represents the problems highlighted in the assessment.

- a supervision plan. This includes an individual programme for the offender, specifying objectives and proposed methods.[1]

- a quarterly progress form. POs record how far existing objectives have been achieved, methods used, and details of any new or modified objectives. Depending on the service, details about breach, compliance, transfer, termination, professional constraints and additional convictions are also included.

- a self-completion questionnaire for offenders, called "How Do You See Things Going?". It asks them about potential problems (e.g. Where I live, My use of drugs) and their relation to offending. It also gauges attitudes towards offending by asking offenders to agree or disagree with a number of statements, e.g. I could stop offending if I wanted to; I am to blame for the offences I was

---

[1]   The Warwickshire and Hereford and Worcester versions also specified nature and frequency of contact and timescale for achieving objectives. The Warwickshire and West Midlands versions included a general analysis of factors based on the assessment form. The Hereford and Worcester version of the supervision plan and quarterly progress also monitored National Standards.

convicted of. There are also some items related to attitude towards supervision. The Hereford and Worcestershire version contained some extra items, including a section about offenders' own experience of victimisation.

Officers in Warwickshire also complete a form at termination, which includes questions on whether the order achieved what was intended, and which methods were seen as successful or unsuccessful. Other information, such as details about the offender and the order, or amendments to the initial assessments, were collected at different points depending on the administration of the service.

(iii)   Case Management Instrument (CMI)

The Kent CMI was piloted in two teams in Kent Probation Service (KPS) in April/May 1998, and was only introduced on a service-wide basis in October 1998. A copy of the form is included in Appendix D. Interviews took place with members of the two pilot teams a month after its introduction.

The CMI approach to needs assessment is similar to that of LSI-R. However, it is not a stand-alone form in the same sense, as it is designed to fit in with Kent procedures. The CMI is started at PSR stage and for all new commencements, but is completed on an ongoing basis throughout the order. There are several components to the form:

- A Risk Assessment Profile, which includes:

- A risk of re-offending scale. Relevant factors (offender factors e.g. age and sex; present offence; needs) predictive of re-offending are assigned scores (e.g. age 17-21 is given the score +4; present offence being criminal damage is given the score −1). These scores are then added up to give a total risk of re-offending score. Scores are pre-banded into low, medium and high. These factors and weightings were derived from an analysis of cases from the Kent area.

- Seriousness rating scale. Relevant factors to the seriousness of the offence (e.g. number of additional offences/tics; currently on bail or in custody) are allotted scores. These are added up to give a final seriousness score, which is pre-banded into low; low-medium; medium-high; high. Offenders with seriousness scores of 18 or over should be considered for county group-work programmes.

- A PSR proposal matrix. This combines the two previous measures to suggest a proposal for sentence.

- A dangerousness/risk of harm checklist. This lists 24 factors to be taken into consideration when assessing dangerousness/harm (e.g. violent behaviour; sex offender; refusal to take medication). Staff can indicate whether the focus of the behaviour is self; staff; public; specific; children; other.

- Case management plans, one for each year of supervision, with reviews carried out at three-monthly intervals. Officers are asked to indicate offenders' motivation to change (high; fair; slight; very little). They also rate strength of needs (slight; moderate; severe) for six 'criminogenic needs' (e.g. lack of prosocial skills, drug abuse) and 12 'other factors/circumstances' (e.g. relationship problems, no/low income, employment issues). The list of criminogenic needs consisted of factors "identified by research as being significantly linked to offending". For each need rated, officers also fill in a case management code, indicating who is to do the work to tackle this (e.g. PO, external resource).

(iv)   Assessment Framework (AF)

The Berkshire Probation Service (BPS) Assessment Framework (AF) was piloted in 1996. It has been in use in BPS since September 1997, although there have been revisions of the tool since its introduction.

The AF represents a very different approach to risk/needs assessment to the other instruments. It does not directly seek to structure the assessment. Instead, officers are asked to specify which outcomes they will target in order to reduce the likelihood of offending. Paperwork is kept to a minimum.

The form itself comprises three distinct components:

- Compliance. Officers fill in details about compliance with National Standards, i.e. the promptness of the first interview, the frequency of contacts in the first three months of supervision, and details about enforcement.

- Reducing the Likelihood of Offending. Officers specify up to six outcomes needed over the period of supervision. In separate sections they also specify outcomes currently targeted, and outcomes achieved. The outcomes are taken from a reference list grouped into the following factors: accommodation, addictive behaviour, attitude orientation, cognitive skills, employment, finance, health, recreation, and relations with others. Examples of specific outcomes are "100: person is in satisfactory accommodation"; "417: person is less aggressive"; "509: person has completed a Number Power programme". Certain outcomes are linked to referral to specific programmes (for example, the CHASE programme currently operating in Berkshire) or assessments (for example, Morrisby assessments).

- Managing the risk of dangerousness behaviour. Officers indicate on the form whether an offender exhibits a "significant risk of dangerous behaviour, either to the public, to staff or to self" on a range of factors.

Officers are expected to re-assess offenders' needs every three months using the AF. A copy of the form and reference lists is in Appendix E.

Structure of the report

Chapter two focuses on how officers used the instruments in their work. Chapter 3 covers training. Chapter 4 looks at the strengths and weaknesses of each instrument as assessed by probation officers, while Chapter 5 looks at potential benefits and problems for their use by middle managers. Chapter 6 concentrates on supplementary tools used alongside these instruments and their suitability for all offenders. Chapter 7 discusses the link to assessing risk of harm and dangerousness. Chapter 8 concludes with implications of the study and makes some recommendations for implementation of the new system.

2   Using the instruments: the practitioner's perspective

This chapter concentrates on how practitioners used the instruments in their work. It first describes what POs thought was the main purpose of the instruments. It then looks in detail, first at how POs employed ACE, LSI-R and CMI at different stages in their work with offenders, and secondly at how the AF was used by officers. (The AF is looked at separately, because of the very different approach it takes.) The chapter ends by examining a a number of other aspects of 'user-friendliness', such as whether a computerised version of the instruments was available.

Main purpose of the instruments

Officers were asked what they saw as the main purpose or purposes of the instruments they used. (Officers often gave more than one.)

In the LSI-R sample, about a third (7 out of 22) of the officers said that LSI-R was a dual assessment, or assessment tool for risks and needs. Just under half (9) the officers thought it fulfilled this function for risk only, and two with needs only. However, three officers saw it as a tool for management, not one for practitioners: *"I think it's probably going to be used to direct resources one way or another but we certainly haven't been told"*. Other responses were that it was meant to make assessments consistent (1), that it helped determine levels of supervision (1) and that it was a means of engaging offenders (1). The SPOs' responses mirrored these with 3 saying it was a dual assessment of risk and needs, 4 that it was for risk of re-offending and 1 that it was for needs. 3 mentioned its use in managing resources, and 1 officer also said it was useful for looking at offenders' progress and for demonstrating effectiveness.

Over half (11 out of 18) the officers using ACE said its main purpose was to help them in some way with assessments, including focusing on relevant areas and in making them more consistent. Two officers said it was specifically to help them assess risk (one specified risk of re-offending and risk of harm). A third (6) said it was to help them look at progress and evaluate how effective their practice was. Four officers thought ACE informed their decisions about what to do with offenders, including the supervision plan. Other suggestions were that it was a way to engage with the offender (2 responses), for case recording (1) and providing an integrated system for the officer (1). One officer said that ACE was for *"pigeonholing people into boxes"* and another that it was *"a paper exercise to prove that we're doing our job... for the inspectors' benefit"*. The SPOs interviewed were broadly in line with this: [4] thought it helped POs with assessments, [2] thought it informed decisions about what to do with offenders and [1] saw it as a means of evaluating practice. Other responses were that it was a dual assessment of risk and needs ([1]), an assessment of needs ([1]) and that it provided an integrated system ([1]).

The main purpose or purposes of the CMI was seen by four of the five POs interviewed as assisting in risk assessment. One officer also mentioned its role in assessing dangerousness. Three officers saw it as improving case management, for example *"to enhance all aspects of case management, and to make better use of a probation officer's time and resources"*. Another officer saw the aim of the CMI as giving *"a quick and visual sense of potential problems... it contributes to the assessment of somebody but it most certainly is not the be all and end all"*.

For the Berkshire AF, one officer recited the three aims of recording compliance, reducing the likelihood of re-offending and managing the risk of harm. One other officer said it was a risk assessment, while four focused on the structure it gave to their work, for example, *"it's like a map for an order"*; *"it informs headquarters of what we do and where we're going, in particular what has been done"*; *"trying to achieve certain outcomes with offenders and set targets so that you know where the work, which way the work is heading"*.

Use of ACE, LSI-R and CMI

(i)   At the PSR stage

The heaviest use of the instruments was at the PSR stage. All the services using LSI-R required officers to complete assessments at the PSR stage. Only two of the 22 LSI-R users did not use LSI-R themselves at the PSR stage, and this was because they did not write PSRs. All the Kent officers started the CMI at the PSR stage. Most (13 out of 18) of the ACE officers used the initial assessment forms at the PSR stage, and all but one of these officers said they "always" used the assessment form for offenders. (For details of how officers actually used the forms to carry out assessment, see sub-section (v).) The five exceptions to doing the assessment at PSR stage were officers in West Midlands, where a service level decision had been taken to complete ACE after the PSR stage. It was felt that a full ACE assessment was too time-consuming at this stage, given that not all PSRs would result in a community sentence.

Most officers (10) using the ACE assessment at the PSR stage said it could contribute to the PSR in a number of ways (even though they did not always consider it to have substantially affected their proposals): *"it's food for thought, it's a framework, it expands the mind a little bit, makes you look at areas that perhaps you wouldn't immediately think about"*; *"[ACE] underpins it really... it forms the basis for that assessment and proposal"*; *"[the form] with some of the evidence boxes would contribute to my thinking about a particular aspect before the report"*; *"I tended to use them more after the event really... to... check through the proposal to see if it related to the ACE form"*. In the other three cases, it was unclear how it contributed. Overall, five officers found it "very useful" at the PSR stage and five said it was "fairly useful". Only one officer said it was "not very useful" at this stage. Two officers could not say. Six officers also used the self-completion offender questionnaire at the PSR stage (see sub-section (vi) for details of how they administered this).

All POs completed the CMI at the PSR stage, and had found it either very (3) or fairly (2) useful at this stage. All of them said that it fed into the PSRs in a variety of ways, by keeping the officer focused (2), acting as a checklist for the assessment (2), as a guide to assessing risk (2) and in assessing the seriousness of the offence (1).

By contrast, the LSI-R sample was split in how useful they found the instrument at the PSR stage: half found it "very" or "fairly" useful (4 and 7 respectively), while for three officers it was "not very useful" and for another three "not at all useful". Half the officers (11) said that LSI-R did not help them write the PSR at all, and these officers were often unhappy with this situation: *"I don't use the form at all to help me do a PSR, it's just a nuisance that I have to fill afterwards because the management want it"*. Eight officers said that LSI-R could contribute to the PSR in a variety of ways, including *"it might highlight bits that you wouldn't have asked"*; *"highlights areas of importance"*; *"useful guideline, almost a checklist"*; *"it helps me structure the interview"*; *occasionally I do it at the end [of the PSR] and then use it as a check and work backwards"*. However, even amongst those officers who said that LSI-R did contribute to the PSR, there was still a feeling that *"there's actually not a lot of difference in the actual PSR produced, pre-LSI-R and now"*. Two officers did not use it at the PSR stage and in one case it could not be established how much the LSI-R contributed.

(ii)   At the start of supervision and input to supervision planning

Broadly speaking, LSI-R assessments were only done at the start of an order if one had not been done at the PSR stage, for example, for cases transferred from another service or on throughcare cases. Four officers said they used LSI-R at the start of an order, and one each at the start of licenses and during transfers. In one service, officers filled in a one-page review sheet at the start of an order. The situation was similar for the Kent CMI, where the main assessment took place at the PSR stage. All the services using ACE had an amendment form which could be used at the start of supervision, to record any changes between the initial assessment and the start of an order. Officers in West Midlands had the additional task at this stage of completing the initial assessment.

The ACE system also includes a supervision plan which should be informed by the initial assessment. All but one of the officers always used this plan. One officer said s/he never used it. Fourteen officers agreed that the initial assessment had input to the supervision plan. This happened in a variety of ways: *"this [initial assessment] document should inform your objectives"; "it's... part of the process, also taking into account what's happened at court, any new information"; "in theory things that are pointing to the most serious bit [in the initial assessment] are the things you know that you need to work on"; "the [supervision plan] is like a very condensed version and I mean very condensed version of [the initial assessment] because it's highlighting what I have assessed as high."* Only two officers said ACE did not help them write the supervision plan. In two cases it was unclear how much the initial assessment fed into the supervision plan. Five officers said they found ACE "very useful" in supervision planning, and six found it "fairly useful". One officer said it was "not very useful", while one said it was "not at all useful". Nine officers also used the self-completion questionnaire at this stage.

The CMI was also felt by most officers (4 out of 5) to contribute to the supervision plan, and was seen as "very" (2 responses) or "fairly" (1) useful. Two officers did not feel they had enough experience to comment on its utility at this stage. In general the CMI was felt to highlight relevant problems to be addressed in supervision, which also helped one officer in setting objectives. One officer said it was useful in engaging the offender, because *"you're going through it with the client and they're actually participating"*. One officer used the CMI as a check on the offender's supervision plan, to *"remind me... is there anything I've missed here"*.

The input of LSI-R into supervision planning was more mixed. Two officers found it "very useful" in supervision planning, while six found it "fairly useful". Two officers said it was "not very useful". Eight officers said that LSI-R contributed in some way to supervision planning (or the plan itself). Again, this could happen in a number of ways:

- *"When we are looking at what to offer the offender we would do so with reference to the LSI. So... the most common there is alcohol and drugs. So we have an alcohol and drug facility in this office. So we would obviously refer them on. Accommodation, we have somebody here and so forth. So it should flag up areas that need attention."*

- *"I'll pick [up the LSI-R] from the court team and check out the areas with the person when I'm preparing a supervision plan."*

Eight officers said that the LSI-R did not contribute to supervision planning. Five of these officers felt this was because the LSI-R form was superseded by the PSR or the supervision plan itself: *"I wouldn't go back really and look at the [LSI-R] form, it's written up in a far more accessible way in the PSR."* Another four officers were not involved in the supervision planning stage at all, and in two cases LSI-R's contribution was unclear.

In three of the services, LSI-R had a major impact on supervision activities as the "Total LSI-R score" was directly used in deciding the level of supervision that an offender was likely to receive. In each of these services, the groupings used were related to local offender profiles. The examples found in the current study were:

- In West Glamorgan, offenders with LSI-R scores of 26+ were eligible for the high risk offender programme. Professional over-ride could be used if there were reasons for not assigning offenders to this programme.

- In Durham, offenders with LSI-R scores of 30+ were initially allocated to the community safety team (more intensive supervision). Those with scores of under 23 were initially allocated to the community supervision team (unless they were deemed a high risk of harm or if professional over-ride had been used). Offenders with scores of 23-29 could be allocated to either community supervision or safety, with reasons specified. Specific mention of drugs/alcohol problems on the LSI-R form was used to trigger referrals to the INTEGRA project.

- In Surrey, the following (provisional) guidelines were suggested for officers: 0-13: low risk ñ minimal reporting scheme; 14-24: medium risk ñ reporting scheme and assessment of criminogenic needs; 25-36: high risk ñ considered for some form of cognitive intervention, considered for RAMAS; 37+: very high risk – should get RAMAS completed. Professional over-ride could be used to give offenders more intensive supervision.

Officers were not specifically asked to comment on what they thought of these strategies, although in one service, there was concern expressed by all the POs interviewed about the choice of cut-off for the high risk offender group. It was felt that *"it throws up too many people as high risk"* and it made people *"go into programmes that they probably don't need"* or were unsuitable, for example, with outstanding drug or alcohol problems. The over-ride was felt to be under-used; one officer thought this was because *"people are afraid to use it, I think, and when they use the over-ride they need to justify it, you know, why they are doing so and I think that tends to put people off then"*.

(iii)   *During the order*

The CMI includes a quarterly review of needs/problems, although four officers using it had no or only limited experience of this. The other officer found it useful in *"being able to clarify what progress the order has... made"* and in *"guiding... what one's doing with the client"*.

All of the services using ACE also carried out quarterly reviews, which looked at how far objectives had been achieved in the last quarter and allowed for any new or modified ones. Fifteen out of the 18 ACE officers had used the quarterly progress forms, although one of them only used them occasionally. Three officers were not involved in or had not yet done such reviews, one because they thought they were a waste of time. (One ACE officer interviewed was only responsible for the PSR and not for supervision of the order.) Full ACE re-assessments (i.e. re-administering the initial assessment form) were carried out every six months in all services but West Midlands, where they were done at the nine-month stage or termination. Ten officers said they had been directly involved in doing ACE re-assessments.

There was more variation between the LSI-R services in how it was used for re-assessment. Two of those using LSI-R did not yet carry out re-assessments, as LSI-R had only recently been introduced, while another two had set six-monthly and termination reviews in place, although very few orders had yet reached the re-assessment stage. In total, seven officers using LSI-R had carried out re-assessments with it, five at the six-monthly stage. Only four officers rated its usefulness in measuring progress: one found it "very" useful, two "fairly" useful and one "not very useful".

Amongst the seven LSI-R users who had experience of re-assessment, three said they had used it to highlight or check areas of improvement. For example, one officer used it in the following way:

> I can actually say [to offenders] "Well look this is what we're working on particularly, this is where you were at and this is where you were scoring or not",

you can share that information with them. And this is the situation now or if it's worse or deteriorated in any way.

However, the other four officers felt that it was of limited use in measuring offenders' progress on an order, and that LSI-R *"doesn't tell you everything, but... it should have a reduced score if you've done something with a person... and if you haven't you need to ask why"*.

- A couple of officers cited the restriction of the tick box format in presenting changes, with the following illustrations:

- *"When somebody's re-offended often that can be sort of a major thing... but the only way the LSI-R form gives any indication of that is that your number of previous convictions go up one from the previous form. But obviously you would be looking at that in a lot of detail: what type of re-offending, why, what was happening you know how they started, been on drinking binge or whatever. You'd be looking at a lot of detail as to why that person had re-offended but the form just, you would have to look quite closely to see that change."*

- *"I have got heroin addicts on my caseload, who use it once a week, where they used to use it every day. But there is still a 'yes there is a problem', you know what I mean? So it is difficult - there is no degree, is there?"*

Half the officers (7 out of 15) who used ACE to check progress found it helpful in a variety of ways: in keeping work on track, in assessing what had been achieved, in identifying changed circumstances and in modifying objectives or methods of working, in following up unachieved objectives. The forms also gave offenders an opportunity to be involved in this process. For example, one officer sometimes re-did the assessment wheel *"because we'll have a picture of the last wheel and they can see for themselves"*. Another worked in the following way:

I tend to fill the review forms in with the offenders - they do it as I do it, they do one copy, I do another copy and that's very good in terms of offender participation really. Quite a friendly way of measuring and taking into account the offender views as well. ... Obviously I would have the final say about where the ticks go in the boxes, but generally I haven't had a problem. Generally we've come to an agreement about progress or not as the case may be.

However, the same number of officers found the use of ACE limited in reviewing progress, mainly because there was a limited amount of change observed *"often the reviews don't change very much"*. Other problems mentioned were burdens of paperwork and that ACE did not add very much to the processes, for example *"I'm not saying that [ACE]'s a significant improvement on what we currently have already because I would expect that kind of information to be put into a supervision plan in any event."* (For one officer, it was unclear how helpful he/she found it.) At this stage, three ACE users found it "very useful", seven "fairly useful" and one "not very useful". In some services, officers also asked offenders to fill in another self-completion questionnaire, but no officers commented about this.

(iv)   At the end of order

There was less information available on what happened at the end of the order. Two services using LSI-R were planning to carry out termination reviews, but few if any relevant orders had expired yet. One of the ACE services carried out another re-assessment at termination, while another had a summary form to be completed at the end of the order.

(v)   Carrying out the actual assessment

This sub-section looks at how the instruments were used to assess offenders, regardless at what stage this was done.

Use of LSI-R in assessment was variable, and depended partly on individual officers' preferences. For about three-quarters (16) of the officers interviewed, their usual practice was to gather the necessary information from offenders during the assessment interviews and fill in the form afterwards. In West Glamorgan, for example, a "pen-picture" had been drawn up which listed the headings from the LSI-R form and served as a topic guide for assessment interviews, rather than the officer filling in the form during the interview. Information was also sometimes taken from files on the offender, and also informed from other sources, for example, other agencies, other offenders and the officers' previous knowledge of individuals. The following officer's practice was typical:

> You tend to do it as you go along with other pieces of work rather than sitting there doing it as a focused piece of work in its own right, because a lot of the information on an LSI-R you would get anyway. There is only a few things you have to sort of actually make a conscious effort to get. ... I think when you start

using it you tend to work with it on your lap sort of thing but as you get into it you know what you are looking for. ...I mean I never ask direct questions. And some of the information you could fill in before you even see them, things like pre-cons, that kind of thing and generally as I say it forms the basis of a lot of the information that you would want in a PSR interview.

The other six officers tended to use the form with the offender during the assessment interview itself. In some cases, this was made an active feature of the interview, in other cases filling in the form was downplayed or just used to confirm or fill in answers that the officer did not already know.

- *"So they [offenders] don't even see it and really I just say, if I know them, I say, 'There are a few questions I'm not clear about', and I run through the form. The form will be there. I don't hide it from them, and then I'll say, 'Were you ever expelled, right, from school', and then I'll say 'You have been employed for a full year haven't you, I remember', then confirm it. So it's that sort of thing. So I don't make a big deal of it. ... So I often try, as I said, to use the information I know and I've got on the file and fill in their other questions [that I] don't know by asking."*

- *"What I do is I say to the person, 'I'm going to ask you about your background and get background information using this questionnaire'. So I ask the questions from the LSI-R questionnaire and mark the questionnaire as I go along, any supplementary information they've put on a pad or paper as I'm doing it or simultaneously. And then while the person's sitting there I tot up the score and I feed that back to them and get their reaction so that it's all done there and then while I'm doing the other tasks."*

Overall, 10 officers said they used the LSI-R form as a general guide to discussion. Three officers used it either as a guide or filled it out question by question, depending on the circumstances, while three only filled it out question by question. However, four officers (all in the group whose usual practice was to fill in the forms after the interview) said they did not use the form in either way, implying it was peripheral to their assessments.

About two-thirds (14 out of 22) of the officers said offenders were not involved in completing the LSI-R form at all, although two officers involved offenders "a lot" and two "quite a lot". When offenders were involved in completing the forms, reactions were generally positive (3 responses) or at least neutral (3). Only one officer said offenders reacted negatively to the form.

ACE users also employed the initial assessment form in a variety of ways, mainly at the PSR stage or at the start of supervision for West Midlands officers. Practice was extremely flexible and depended on the capability and interest of the offender, how well the officer knew them and how accustomed they were to probation. One officer whose practice was variable described the considerations behind how they used the form thus:

> It depends on how used to assessment the person is. I think if it's someone who I think is really used to it and they've been through the process several times, I'll say to them "There's certain areas that I want to cover in the interview that might be relevant to what's happened" and I'll do it that way and I'll have the form and be very open with it and show them with it and discuss it with them. But if it's someone where I do get the sense that it's all very strange to them and they're not really on top of things, they might be shocked or not used to being in that situation, then I'd probably do it more implicitly and have the sort of headings and ideas in my head but not necessarily have the form and say "well what do you think about this?"

Eight officers said their typical practice was to gather information for the ACE assessment during the initial interview and fill out the forms afterwards, for example *"I wouldn't actually do it with the questions with them. But as you go on you tend to remember these things and so you can actually complete it afterwards. But there again, it varies, some people their situation's so complicated, so many things going on, it's sometimes good to have it there and then."* Four officers would often complete parts of the form in the interview. Practice varied from *"I wouldn't directly ask the questions but the way I interview ensures that I've asked all the questions"* to slightly more active involvement: *"for those offenders who like explanations and structure I would share it with them [but they're] not [involved] very much because I'm tending to tell them what I'm writing."* Four officers went through the forms during the interview, for example, *"go through it as it is, going through questions in the order it's in"*, *"I do it quite formally with them and that's what I don't like, because I don't think it helps build a relationship"*. Overall, 10 officers in the ACE sample said that offenders were generally positive about the use of all the ACE forms (not just the initial assessment form). Only two officers said they reacted negatively.

All of the CMI officers used the form as a guide to what they talked about with offenders in interviews, although one said they would also fill it out question by question. Four officers actively referred to the forms during interviews as appropriate. One of these officers said they would not refer to them if it wasn't suitable for particular offenders. Examples of practice were:

- "I usually do [the CMI] after the interview... but the risk of re-offending I often share with the client."

- "you use it as a discussion tool, you'd have to marry it with the individual which you're working to, it's something you use consistently, but it depends because some people are much more receptive and open to discussion and some people [just say] yes, no."

One officer tended to complete the form after s/he had done the interview.

In two cases, officers said offenders were directly involved with the form. Both said that offenders' reactions were usually "fairly positive".

(vi) Administering the ACE self-completion questionnaire

The ACE system also included a self-completion form for offenders. This was intended for use alongside the officers' assessment of an individual, so that both can inform the supervision plan. The self-completion form was used by officers at both the PSR stage, at the start of supervision and by some officers during supervision. In two cases, it was unclear precisely when the officer used the self-completion form. Four officers said they often used the self-completion forms, while one never used it (the other 13 always used it). The way officers used this form depended on the offenders' capabilities and how interested they were in the forms. For seven officers, it was usual practice to let the offenders take the form away or send it to them to complete:

- "I don't do it in the first interview. After that you try to build trust, work on the relationship and then say have a bash at this, take it home, go through it with your partner, your mum, dad, keep it for couple of weeks, if you have any problems get back to me and I'll help you."

- "We've actually now formulated a process where we send that [self-completion] form out with any appointment. If the appointment's given to them verbally at the office here they will have it then or if it's by letter it will go as a letter. ... It's got a surprisingly high return rate, I could hazard 85-90 per cent return rate ... When I say 85-90 per cent completion, they're actually bringing it to the interview and at some point during the interview we would refer to it. I don't like giving people pieces of work and then not acknowledging that they've done it."

Seven officers said they would either let the offender take the form away or would fill it in with them, for example: *"if I think that they can do it on their own then I will let them take it away and do it on their own. But most of them they quite like to fill it in and do it while you're there. But for some people it's far beyond them to sort of sit with you and to go ticking boxes sort of thing, it's better to let them do it and then discuss it afterwards."* Two officers usually filled the self-completion form in with offenders. In three cases, it was unclear how officers used the form.

The form could also be used to initiate discussions with offenders, particularly if there was a discrepancy between officers' and offenders' opinions. In the ACE design, raising and tackling differences between officers' and offenders' perceptions was seen as an important function of the self-completion questionnaire. Seven officers referred to using it like this, for example, *"I do the main ACE assessment first and then ask them to do [the self-completion] and then they compare the two."* One officer had used the self-completion form *"with younger people who often find it difficult to sit in a room and talk to anybody, particularly about things they don't want to talk about like offending. They would rather talk about something else. So to help focus, that's been very useful"*. Six officers said their use of the form was affected by the offender having difficulties reading or writing, for example, *"some can't even write and they get embarrassed"*, *"my biggest difficulty with it is that people are put off because they can't read and often I am not wanting to be up front about that"*, *"if someone has got literacy problems, it takes forever to do"*. Other problems with using the form with offenders were complaints about the amount of paperwork, problems with the layout i.e. *"most people find it quite daunting because there is a lot of information in a small space"*, and a general suspicion of filling out forms.

Use of the AF (outcomes required to reduce the likelihood of re-offending)

This section focuses on use of the Berkshire AF with regard to specifying the outcomes required to reduce the likelihood of offending, as opposed to the sections on compliance or risk of harm. Use of the Berkshire AF could start at the PSR stage. However, only two out of the five officers said they specified the outcomes needed to reduce the likelihood of re-offending at this stage. One of these officers completed this part of the AF after s/he had written the PSR, although s/he said that it still helped the PSR as, because s/he knew s/he had to complete it, it kept them more focused on outcomes. The other officer did not feel that the AF contributed to the PSR, more that *"the PSR can contribute to the assessment framework"*.

The other officers specified outcomes at the start of supervision. One officer completed this part of the AF about two weeks into the start of the order and felt this was a better time because *"I can get a grip on their attitude and because it invariably changes after the PSR"*. One of the officers who did fill out the AF at the PSR stage also mentioned how s/he would often add to the AF at the start of supervision. Overall, three officers said AF was useful at either the PSR or start of supervision phase, while two said it was not useful.

In two cases, it was unclear whether the AF had any direct impact on the assessment itself. However, three of the officers seemed to be using the list of outcomes as a means of structuring or at least checking their assessments, for example, *"[the list of outcomes] is quite helpful just to keep you on track about what we are looking for here and what may be the problems"*.

Four of the officers said that offenders were aware of the form as it was being completed. The other officer had tried initially to use the form with offenders but *"I think people couldn't go with this number thing and I've stopped doing it now because it's just not on."* Only two officers said they directly involved the offender in completing the forms. One said the usual reaction was fairly positive, the other that offenders were indifferent to the use of the form. The main point of contact with the form came in agreeing the outcomes or objectives of supervision. One officer felt that it was difficult to share the forms *"because they don't understand it. What I would probably do is give them verbal guidance through it... they are welcome to see it. ... But it's not like the old Part B where you could say: well, sign this, this is what we are going to do."* (The concern about the transparency of the forms was shared by other officers, see Chapter 4.)

Three of the officers were clear that the AF contributed to supervision planning, in a variety of ways. Two of them said it focused the direction of the supervision, in one case, via the outcomes. The other officer felt that the AF itself was the supervision plan. However, one officer expressed concern that *"the way it's designed, it doesn't really readily give the opportunities for the draw[ing] up of supervision plans"*.

All officers used it for the three-monthly re-assessments, and there was the same 3:2 split with regard to usefulness at this stage. The re-assessment was used for *"comparing the 'outcomes targeted' and whether any of those have been achieved"*. Officers found it useful for the following reasons: it was an opportunity for the officer to review the order and modify outcomes (4); see what outcomes had been achieved (2); check on outcomes that had not been achieved (1); and engage the offender with their progress or congratulate them on their progress (2). There were two main limitations to the AF's use in measuring progress. Three officers felt that the form did not adequately reflect progress, i.e. it only said whether an outcome had been achieved or not. Another officer had a more fundamental problem with the AF in measuring progress because *"it's almost inviting you to say there's some change - you know, to be optimistic, perhaps where there isn't any optimism. ... Because effective changes are [a] very, very time consuming thing and if anybody thinks they can do [it] in a sort of six-months sort of thing, well, it's cloud cuckoo land, isn't it? It's all cumulative"*.

Best times to use instruments

Most officers completing ACE, CMI and LSI-R felt that the PSR stage was one of the best times to complete an assessment (Table 2.1). Smaller numbers favoured assessments at the start of the order, and some specified assessments at the start of licenses. There was some debate about the merits of filling in assessments at the PSR stage or post-PSR. Arguments put forward for doing assessments at PSR stage were that they could then feed into the PSR proposals and subsequent supervision planning, and that it would be available for all offenders, particularly those sentenced to custody who then go on to probation supervision under licenses. Arguments against doing the initial assessment at PSR stage were that there was not enough time available to do a proper assessment or form a relationship of trust with the offender. There was also the suggestion that pre-sentence motivations were very different so that offenders tended to conceal certain problems (e.g. a drugs habit) in case it affected their sentence or agreed to certain activities which they had no real intention of doing.

Table 2.1 Best times to use ACE, LSI-R and CMI: PO sample

	ACE	LSI-R	CMI
PSR stage	11	14	3
Start of supervision	5	4	1
Start of supervision if not at PSR	0	1	0
Re-assessment during supervision:	10	11	0
1 month stage	1	0	0
3 month stage	3	5	1
6 month stage	2	2	0
Period not specified	4	4	0
Termination	2	4	0
Pre-release (license)	1	1	0
Post-release (license)	1	0	2
After significant life event	0	1	0
Total in sample	18	22	5

About half the ACE and LSI-R officers also thought some form of re-assessment should be done during supervision, as did one of the Kent officers. Of these officers, nine thought that this should be done at the three-monthly stage and four at the six-monthly stage. This did not necessarily entail a full re-assessment, some officers thought that a simplified review would be adequate. Four officers using LSI-R and two using ACE thought there should be some re-assessment at termination. (The question was not asked of Berkshire officers.)

Consistency

Officers were asked whether they had taken over cases with assessments made by other officers, and if so, whether they usually agreed with the other officers' assessments. No CMI users and only two ACE-using officers said they usually or sometimes disagreed with other officers' assessments. Two out of the five AF users also said this, and both said this was because of the offender disclosing more and because it was a different officer completing (one also said it was because circumstances had sometimes changed). A higher proportion, about a third (7 out of 22) of LSI-R users disagreed with other officers' assessments. The most common reason given by this group for disagreement (5 responses) was that offenders had disclosed more to the officer since the first assessment.

Overlap with other forms

Most of the CMI users (4) and about half the officers in the other samples (ACE: 7, LSI-R: 10 and AF: 3) felt that there was overlap between information needed for the instruments and other forms. Five officers in the LSI-R sample, two in the CMI and one in the ACE sample mentioned overlap with risk of harm forms. Another complaint by four ACE users and one LSI-R user was the repetition of standard offence and demographic information for each offender on different forms. The Berkshire officers said there was repetition between the AF and information they had to give to PROBIS. Kent was due to rationalise some of its forms, as officers were currently duplicating some information. Three of its officers mentioned overlap with monitoring forms, although these were also mentioned by other users, for example, ethnic monitoring forms. Other forms mentioned as potentially overlapping were Home Detention Curfew forms and PSRs themselves. Some of this overlap could eventually be reduced by computerisation and the introduction of CRAMS.

Computerisation

Computerised versions of the instruments were uncommon. Only four officers in two of the ACE services (Warwickshire and Hereford and Worcester) knew of computerised versions of ACE. However, none of these officers routinely entered information onto the computer, or used it to get information about certain cases.

3

Training

Probation officers were asked about the training they had received in order to use the instruments, and how satisfied they were with it.

All the LSI-R training had been provided by the Cognitive Centre Foundation. Most of the ACE training had been given by the University of Oxford – 12 out of the 18 ACE-using officers said that they had received their training from Oxford. However, two officers said they had been trained to use ACE by colleagues. For the locally developed instruments, there was no formal training. Officers were introduced to the instruments in meetings with their SPOs, senior management staff and, in the case of Kent, research staff.

The majority of officers in the ACE (12 out of 18) and LSI-R (15 out of 22) samples had received more than a day's training in using the instruments (Table 3.1). However, two officers who had recently started using ACE, had not received any formal training, although both would have liked some. One officer was now comfortable with the form but wanted training *"otherwise it's just another form when you are ticking boxes but you are not quite sure why you are ticking the boxes"*. The other still felt *"unequipped"* to complete the assessment properly. Meetings in Kent and Berkshire had usually lasted between two hours up to half a day. One Kent officer had missed this introductory meeting. Two officers in Berkshire also said they had not received any training to complete the AF, although one commented that *"it seems... quite common sense... I didn't think training was necessary"*.

Table 3.1 Length of training: PO sample

	ACE	LSI-R	CMI	AF
Length of training:				
None	2	0	1	2
1 day or less	2	7	4	3
More than 1 day	12	15	0	0
Total	16	22	5	5

Broadly speaking, most officers who had received training were content with the length of their training (Table 3.2).

Table 3.2 Views about training: PO sample

	ACE	LSI-R	CMI	AF
Length of training:				
Enough	10	13	4	3
Too long	3	4	0	0
Too short	1	2	0	0
Content of training:				
Suitable	15	13	3	2
Not suitable	1	9	1	1
Total (who had training)	16	22	4	3

All but one of the ACE officers were happy with the content of the initial training. For example, one officer commented, *"We were given enough information to understand it theoretically and really then what you had to do was put it into practice and then I think you need training as you go along about the issues that come about in the practice."* Suggestions for improvement to the ACE training were: greater use of example material; having effectiveness training prior to ACE training; and being informed about the whole ACE process at the start of the training.

In Kent, the content of the training had been broadly acceptable, although one officer commented that *"we did feed back in writing, but it would have been useful to discuss it again with them, I think."* One of the AF users also felt that a feedback session after a few months of using the AF would have been useful.

Satisfaction with the content of the LSI-R training was much lower: nearly half (9 out of 22) the officers using LSI-R said the content of their training was not suitable. Six officers complained about the use of a video during the training (*"extremely boring"* was one comment). The same number also said there was not enough opportunity to answer officers' queries or concerns about the instrument: *"it was more or less a presentation"; "the trainer was very closed off to taking on board our points of view about how we felt or what we felt was the usefulness of the form"*. Five officers thought that the training was too slow, and the same number that it was too "Canadian". Other comments were that there should have been more hands-on practice (3 officers), that it should have been more detailed (3), that it did not engage officers (2), there was no opportunity to use forms and discuss the results (2), that explanations were unclear (2), that the training was repetitive (1) or too commercial (1). One officer stressed that it was important for the training to *"make it seem like this is really going to be useful to [officers] and that just didn't happen"*.

Training forms a crucial part of the introduction of such assessment tools to a service. For many officers, it constitutes the first encounter with the new instruments. It can also have a role in setting the stage for them, by addressing officers' concerns or wider cultural issues within the service that might have a bearing on how instruments are received and implemented. Interviewees were not specifically asked to comment about how the assessment tools were received within their service or about resistance to them, but some officers did talk about this stage. Edited accounts from officers in four different services are given below.

Account 1: LSI-R (PO and SPO)

In the beginning there were big differences between our assessments and assessments made by others. ... I think they weren't delving deep enough, they weren't doing it properly basically. I don't know whether it's down to the lack of training or whether they just didn't want to do it and there was a lot of resistance to using LSI-R at the beginning. (PO)

It's a huge cultural shift to get officers to use an assessment tool, so there has been a large amount of resistance to using this particular tool. To try and find reasons for that is not always very clear, whether it's resistance to the time it takes, actually learning how to use it and implement it effectively. There are a lot of reasons and officers came up with all sorts of reasons, like: oh well ACE is much better, it's much more simple, user-friendly and of course there is a resistance also because [LSI-R]'s not designed to be used for sex offenders and [we] manage quite a large number of sex offenders in my team. ... So there were practical implications for the use of and interpretation of [LSI-R] as well as a cultural resistance.

I think some staff are still afraid of using it as a tool because it looks a lot of information to gather, I do think that it's probably a training issue. That staff need to be talking through in a safe arena about their feelings of inadequacies completing a form. How they ask the questions, the intonation in the voice, the body language that goes with it. ... It isn't simply: here's an inventory, ask these questions, it's not as straightforward as that. The managers have just got to keep plugging away at it and keep pushing that it is a consistent tool and that's where I'm coming from. That it may not be the best tool we have at the moment, but it's the only consistent tool. (SPO)

Account 2: LSI-R (SPO)

There was a group of people who were quite hostile to it and that was because it wasn't being seen as a tool that enhances or confirms what you were thinking. And it was almost as if: well, if you need this, you don't need us... so I think a lot of it is about getting people to own it and to see the advantages of it.

The criticisms that came out were... these are the sorts of things we would have known anyway, these are the sorts of things we would have asked about. I mean people found it insulting when it was first brought in, I think that's fair to say. I think that's unfortunate because I think it was - this is going to sound awful - but it was 'sold' to us in two ways: one, financial, but it was sold to us by the delivery i.e. the training. It was a hard sell and that was because [there] was... a cost to it. So you felt like you were being sold a car and therefore it wasn't being... delivered in a way that maybe people would have listened more to it. ... [People's] concerns about how, what good is this to us... would have been met in a different way and I felt that wasn't actually met and a lot of those feelings weren't dealt with. So I think when it was introduced with a number of groups it actually left a nasty taste in people's mouth which would have caused me concern as the manager for the court team, thinking are people going to sabotage it, are people not really going to do it, are they not going to own it. And I think that in the first infancy... that may well have been happening because people were choosing not to complete it. I think, now that it actually has significance in our structure [note: scores linked to levels of supervision], people can see more of a reason for it. ... So it's this gradual phased introduction of the concept of it and the usefulness of it and which I suppose comes through line management more than anything. ... But people... did it because they had to at one point. Now people... are looking and thinking, yeah, well, hang on their score is that but but there are these, these, these and these factors. ... I think that reflects people's response to change generally because it was a huge structural change [note: service also underwent re-structuring] and I think it would have been too much for people to take on the conceptual things. I think they just had to use it as a tool and get into the process of just using it.

I think if you ask staff members if they could get rid of it tomorrow they might still say, yes, but I think that's the response in terms of filling in paperwork and bureaucracy. ... People are at that point where they are starting to recognise that it has significance. I think that's maybe because as a service we've chosen to give its significance and quite strong significance.

Account 3: ACE (SPO and 2 POs)

Initially... a lot of [officers] thought it was going to be really good and they were really looking forward to using it. And then I think - whether it was because of a lack of training or whatever or lack of timing - I think you do need to actually get into the form quite a lot before you use it or you use it constructively. And I suppose they did moan about it, I'm not sure you want that answer. And because it was a pilot there were lots of thing wrong with it, so things have been changing. But people who used it over a period of time have actually said that it is good if you can get into it but it's not using it all in one go, it's actually having... it there and using it throughout with the clients. (SPO)

The field officers, including myself, became quite demotivated at the second day of training when lots of other forms were introduced... and I was the co-ordinator of the project in this team. (PO 1)

Initially [the problems were] well how... do you use this form? ... And the fact there was some people that were virtually going through it by rote. And so we had a discussion in the team meeting about... the best way forward to actually use the form and what I was saying to them... [was]... that you can use it as a tool in assessments and it's there, so you use it every time you see the client you don't just use it once. (SPO)

Set in context that [when ACE was introduced] we were at a time then where our staff was plummeting, the work was going the other way and I couldn't give a stuff to be honest it just seemed like something more to do on top [of] what we were already doing and when it was pushed to the pilot project it was something on top of rather than instead of. [Now] the staff [have got] more familiar with it because it is comfortable to use it instead of what we used to use before it (PO 2).

Account 4: ACE (SPO and 4 POs)

I suppose at the time [it was introduced] there was some - well there is with any change - people weren't particularly keen on it. It's not as if it was the whole service was wanting to go for it, but who does like change? But it was one of these things you were told, you're going to have to do it. People have to come along and learn it really. (PO 1)

[At the training] certain officers that had been involved in the pilots were kind of trained and they just shared their experiences. (PO 1)

I think we found there was everything, so many changes at the same time and no time to absorb, try out, question, check out how to use the system, consequently I think a lot of people are using it in an inappropriate way. (PO 2)

Originally the thoughts came from Oxford and perhaps with talking with probation. But *[in the next phase] we came back and said, well, I don't think that's right, we are not going to get issues, we need to reframe that and so as it's gone on its got better. ... Now we have... a practice development group for the system and we are modifying [the forms]. Even yesterday we made some decisions about changing the forms, changing the language and asking more pertinent questions. (PO 1)*

I've been part of a group... which was looking at... improving the system, so training in that respect with colleagues, peer training, but then also more formal training as it was introduced to the service. (PO 3)

We've moved through implementing the actual assessment into problems with formulating SMART objectives and now we are actually meeting the problems that are coming up with the... supervision plan reviews. [This] is really a reflection of the implementation process... where in some cases we are twelve months on. (SPO)

[I'm] very happy about the assessment element and not... quite so happy about the case recording, evaluation aspect, and I think that would reflect the... development phases as well. I mean there's more development done on the assessment bit than on the rest. (PO 4)

There have been developmental problems which we've tackled as we've gone along. And we are reviewing the forms just now and that'll mean that we can benefit from other services, our experience of using them as well and in terms of alterations that we need to make. (SPO)

It's been quite a long process in terms of getting to this for all that it is. It's been tested quite a lot really. (PO 3)

4   Strengths and weaknesses of the instruments

This chapter first compares the perceived strengths and weaknesses of the four instruments: ACE, LSI-R, AF and CMI, as identified by the POs using them. It then looks at how POs rated each instrument's utility in a number of different aspects of their work.

Strengths

Table 4.1 shows an overview of the perceived strengths of each instrument, as identified by the POs using them. For all the instruments, apart from the Berkshire AF, the main benefit was felt to be the added improvement to the officers' assessment - nearly all of the ACE, LSI-R and CMI users cited one or more ways that the tool had improved their assessments. Similar numbers also said the instruments had a useful input into supervision planning. However, over two-thirds of the officers in the ACE sample said that ACE was useful for working with offenders (compared to very small numbers for the other instruments). Over half of the LSI-R users thought that their instrument made the process seem more scientific and credible in some way, compared to under a third of the ACE sample, two out of five of the CMI users and no Berkshire officers. Three out of the five POs interviewed in Kent said that the tool helped in the supervision process itself. The very different nature of the Berkshire AF showed itself in its perceived strengths: it was seen by most officers interviewed as helping in supervision planning and in the supervision process, and as being quick to complete.

Table 4.1 Strengths of ACE, LSI-R, CMI and AF: PO sample

	ACE	LSI-R	CMI	AF
Improves officers' assessment in some way	**14**	**19**	**4**	**2**
Acts as checklist or aide-memoire for assessment/ makes assessments more thorough	9	11	3	1
Focuses on/highlights relevant areas for assessment	9	7	3	1
Gives a structure for assessment interview/assessment tool	9	6	0	1
Helps you ask difficult questions/areas	8	4	1	0
Makes assessments more consistent	5	6	0	0
Makes you ask questions officer would have missed otherwise	1	5	0	1
Can challenge officers' assessment/thinking	2	4	1	0
Differentiates between criminogenic and non-criminogenic needs/problems	3	0	0	0
Added time it takes is worth it because of improvements to assessment	2	1	1	0
Gives a structure for analysis/thinking	1	1	1	0
Improves supervision planning in some way	**13**	**10**	**4**	**4**
Focuses on/highlights issues to be addressed as identified in assessment	4	8	3	2
Helps officer decide type of supervision/level of intervention/write supervision plan	6	2	1	0
Improves specification of objectives	5	0	1	0
Helps officer decide sentence/write PSR	3	1	2	0
Aids referral out to other programmes/resources	0	2	2	0
Makes level of service/intervention to offenders more consistent	2	0	1	0
Helps focus on outcomes	0	0	0	2
Triggers other assessments/investigations	1	1	1	0
Helps justify giving low risk offender lower sentence	0	0	1	0
Useful tool for working with offender	**13**	**3**	**1**	**1**
Can use to engage with offender/raise issues or problems with offender	11	3	1	0
Starting point, contract, mandate etc for offender	3	1	1	0
Opportunity for offender to give their own views	3	0	0	0
Can use to discuss progress with offender	1	1	0	1
Useful as introduction for offender	0	1	0	0

Makes process more scientific, credible, quantifiable	5	11	2	0
Provides evidence/validation/confirmation to officer for assessment or suggested activities	2	5	0	0
Provides evidence/validation/credibility for assessment to demonstrate to others e.g. the public, the courts	2	5	0	0
Makes assessment more formal/scientific/objective	2	3	0	0
Provides quantifiable/numerical estimate of risk or needs	1	2	0	0
Having a number/final score is useful	0	2	0	0
Based on local research	0	0	2	0
Makes officer accountable for assessment	1	1	0	0
Improves supervision process in some way	**8**	**1**	**3**	**4**
Can measure/demonstrate offenders' progress	7	1	2	0
Gives structure for supervision	5	0	2	3
Focus on what work needs to be done during supervision	3	0	1	2
Helps in case management	0	0	2	0
Keeps enforcement in mind	0	0	0	1
Provides information about a case in some way	**7**	**7**	**1**	**3**
Provides summary of case/broad picture	1	5	1	3
Professional over-ride/notes/evidence boxes are good	4	2	0	0
Case recording	3	0	0	0
Gives a common language	0	1	0	0
Useful to have prior assessment on an offender	0	1	0	0
Helps management/service	**1**	**6**	**0**	**0**
Helps service management to allocate resources, determine programmes etc	0	5	0	0
Probation service needs one tool	0	3	0	0
Helps supervisors	1	1	0	0
Miscellaneous	**8**	**12**	**3**	**4**
Makes assessment quicker/more time for other things	1	1	0	4
Form is easy, simple to fill in	2	3	1	1
Useful for new officers	1	3	0	0
Makes boundary between high-low risk clearer, useful for borderline cases	0	3	0	0
Ties in with What Works training	0	0	2	0
Improves time management	0	1	0	0
Measure of other factors that probation can't affect	0	1	0	0
Highlights links between factors	0	1	0	0
Other	8	4	1	0
Total	**18**	**22**	**5**	**5**

The next section looks in more detail at each of the main benefits listed in the table.

(i)   *Improving assessments*

Most of the users of LSI-R (19 out of 22), ACE (14 out of 18) and CMI (4 out of 5) said that the tool they used helped assessments in some way. By contrast, only two officers using the Berkshire AF felt it improved the assessment itself - unsurprising as it did not specifically seek to structure the assessment interview.

- One of the main advantages cited by all groups (11 LSI-R, 9 ACE and 3 CMI users) was that the instruments acted as a check-list for the assessment, so that they covered all the relevant areas more thoroughly.[2] *"I think you get more information using LSI than you would otherwise"; "in an interview, for example you can sometimes forget certain areas, when you are rushed or distracted but [ACE] certainly helps in terms of that"; "[CMI] provides a very clear basis of areas which perhaps you'd miss in ordinary interviewing techniques".*

- Half the ACE users (9), about a third (7) of the LSI-R-using officers and four of the CMI users also said the instruments kept them focused on relevant areas for assessment[3] , for example, *"[LSI-R] highlights the main areas, I think, underlying offending behaviour and allows you then to focus in on those"; "In the good old days when I started, you know, the PSR rambled on about all sorts of things, you know, I've two dogs and a chum so on and so forth and lots of irrelevant information, and I think the ACE form does home in on problems and offending behaviour".*

- Nine ACE users and six LSI-R users felt that the tools gave structure to the interview or operated as an assessment tool: *"it's the questions I would ask anyway but it's just done in a sequence that I can just run through [LSI-R]."* None of the CMI users cited this as an advantage.

---

2 Areas that LSI-R helped in particularly were emotional/personal (2), alcohol and drugs (1), criminal history (1), marital/family (1), education (1), finance (1) and attitudes. One officer using ACE mentioned motivation/attitudes to supervision. One officer using CMI mentioned remorse, motivation, violence, abuse and drug and alcohol abuse.

3 Areas mentioned for LSI-R (once each) were criminal history, companions, marital/family, education, financial and attitudes.

- Eight ACE users said that the forms helped them to ask difficult questions. The most common areas cited by officers were sexual behaviour (3), experience of discrimination (2), holding discriminatory attitudes (2), relationships/family (2), attitudes (2) and lifestyle (2)[4]. By comparison, only four LSI-R users said LSI-R was beneficial in this way. One officer using CMI said it helped them to ask questions about mental health, domestic violence, child protection issues, racial motivation and learning disabilities.

- Six officers in the LSI-R sample said it made assessments more consistent. This was seen as an advantage by five of the ACE users, but none of the CMI users.

- Five officers said LSI-R made them ask questions about things they would have missed otherwise. Examples cited were criminal history and companions (2 responses each)[5]. Another advantage cited by four officers in the LSI-R sample was that LSI-R could help to challenge an officers' thinking on a case. Three ACE users said that one benefit of ACE lay in how it helped them to differentiate between criminogenic and non-criminogenic needs, so that for example "if someone's gone out and committed a violent assault it's much easier to make sure that those objectives focus on the reasons the person's offending and not just on getting them somewhere to live or some of the non-criminogenic need".

(ii) Improving supervision planning

LSI-R was seen as having a role in supervision planning by 10 officers who used it, as was ACE by 13 officers using it. CMI was helpful in this way to four officers, and the AF to four officers too. The main benefit of LSI-R and CMI was that it focused on or highlighted which issues needed to be addressed (8 LSI-R users and 3 CMI users). Two AF users also said it helped in focusing the assessment. One LSI-R officer talking about drugs and alcohol said "this brings [them] out as being particularly relevant and if you highlight them properly you can actually use this as a referral system." However, only four ACE officers thought that ACE contributed to supervision planning in this way. ACE was seen by six officers as having more use in helping the officer to write the supervision plan – "once you get the hang of [ACE], the supervision plan should write itself". Five officers said that ACE improved

---

4   Other areas mentioned for ACE were self-abuse (1), domestic violence (1), friends (1), experience of homophobia (1), effects on victims (1).

5   Also mentioned for LSI-R were emotional/personal (1), alcohol/drug (1), companions (1), employment (1), finance (1) and the participation/performance/interaction questions (1).

objectives, making them *"more specific and explicit"* and *"SMART"* (standing for specific, measurable, achievable, realistic and timescale attached). Two out of the five CMI users also said the CMI helped them in writing the PSR and in aiding referral out to other agencies. Two of the AF users said it helped them to focus on desired "outcomes" of the order, which they were required to specify by the start of supervision.

(iii)   Useful tool for working with offender

There was a marked contrast between the instruments in how many officers saw them as a tool for working with offenders directly. Over two-thirds (13 out of 18) of the ACE-using officers said ACE brought benefits in this way, with 11 saying that it could be used to engage with the offender in some way, to raise issues or problems or initiate discussion with them. Seven officers were referring here to the self-completion document, while three thought the assessment wheel was also useful here, for example, *"[the wheel] can be good for the PSR stage for translating what's going on for the actual offender."* One officer was referring to the attitudes and victim awareness section of the initial assessment. Three officers also said it was useful for the offender to give their own viewpoint, while the same number saw the forms as a good starting point for an order or license, when agreement and boundaries could be established. However, only three officers using LSI-R, one using CMI and one using the AF thought that they were useful in working with offenders directly.

(iv)   Making process more scientific/credible

LSI-R was seen, by half the LSI-R users interviewed, as a more objective, scientific, numerical process. LSI-R's main strengths were seen as providing credibility to officers' assessments. This worked at two levels. One, it could provide back-up to the officers' own gut feelings about a case (5 responses), with one officer saying *"it's quite good to have your opinions affirmed by a score"*. Secondly it could be used to provide evidence or back-up for officers' assessments to others, for example, the courts, the public, the offender or the Home Office (5 responses). One LSI-R user referred to the current climate in courts: *"Whereas in the past perhaps we've said, well, I felt, I thought, you know that at least we've got something solid behind us. It feels better when you're standing up in court and there's a challenge and it's one of your reports."* As another officer put it, *"I don't think that we don't have those skills to make those assessments, but I think we need to prove to somebody that we do have them."*

By contrast, only five ACE users and none of the Berkshire officers mentioned this as an advantage. Two officers using CMI mentioned the benefit of it being based on local research, one of whom felt that *"if we use something like this, it's got to be based on pertinent research that fits the offender profiles in this country"*.

(iv)   Improving supervision process

Only one officer saw LSI-R as impacting on the supervision process directly, and this was in establishing an offenders' progress on an order/license. However eight officers using ACE said that it was helpful here, as did four of the AF and three of the CMI users. The main benefits were that it provided a means of measuring or demonstrating offenders' progress on an order (7 ACE and 2 CMI), and that it provided a structure for supervision itself (5 ACE, 3 AF and 2 CMI). One of the AF users mentioned its ability to *"break down the objectives into small parts so that they seem... clear and achievable."* Three ACE and two AF officers also said that it helped officers and offenders focus on what work needed to be done during supervision, while two of the CMI sample mentioned its role in aiding case management.

(v)   Providing information about a case

Seven officers in the ACE and LSI-R groups and three using the AF saw the instruments as useful in providing information about a case. However, most of the officers using LSI-R (5), the AF (3) and the CMI (1) said it was useful in giving a summary of an individual, which *"you can scan quickly to find out what you want as a first port of call. [LSI-R]"* One AF user said they *"could compare it with either reading a book or reading the list of contents."* Four officers using ACE said that filling in the notes/evidence boxes was useful as *"it's the opportunity to give some evidence"*, and three that it aided case recording.

(vi)   Helps management/service

Six officers saw LSI-R as being useful for management. Most (5) cited its use in helping management to allocate and target resources, to establish levels of service for different types of offender and determine what programmes were needed. One officer saw the *"need to start quantifying these matters and sort of working in a more consistent and logical fashion I suppose, asking what is the role of the probation service in today's society, who should we be aiming to supervise, where should our resources be going into."* Only one ACE officer and none of the CMI or AF users said that the instruments they used had a role in this respect.

(vii)   *Other benefits*

One of the main benefits of the AF, cited by four officers, was that it made the assessment quicker, mainly because there was less paperwork and administration to complete.

Other benefits of the instruments were seen as the form being easy to fill in (ACE and LSI-R), being useful for new officers (LSI-R), being useful for border-line cases (LSI-R) and in fitting in with What Works training (CMI).

Weaknesses

Given the basic differences in the design of ACE, LSI-R, CMI and AF, the problems associated with the instruments were slightly different, although these have been grouped into similar themes. Table 4.2 shows the main weaknesses and problems of the instruments, as described by the POs using them.

Overall, the main weaknesses of LSI-R were that officers had problems filling in existing questions on the form, the form was not felt to help POs in their work, LSI-R missed or under-covered some areas, forms were limited and officers had problems with the concept or inclusion of some items. By contrast, the main concerns with ACE were that it was burdensome to complete, there were problems filling in the form and forms were limited. The main problems with CMI were concerns with limitations of forms and problems filling in existing items on the form. The Berkshire AF had one main criticism, concerned with limitations of the form.

The next section looks in detail at the main problems associated with the instruments.

(i)   *Problems filling in the form*

One of the main areas of concern with LSI-R was that officers had problems when they were filling in the forms. The most common problems are described below, the main one being the use of ambiguous or unclear wording (including jargon), cited by 13 officers. The main difficulties with LSI-R here were:

- the distinction between the terms "friends" and "acquaintances" in items 33 to 36, both officers and offenders had trouble with this.

- the wording of the item "unfavourable towards convention" "an unbelievable statement. I mean really whose convention are we talking [about]."

Table 4.2 Weaknesses of ACE, LSI-R, CMI and AF: PO sample

	ACE	LSI-R	CMI	AF
Problem filling in existing items on form	13	18	4	0
Language/meaning vague/unclear	5	13	0	0
Language is too "American"	–	9	–	–
Uses double negatives	0	7	0	0
Items/coding too subjective	6	3	0	0
Reliance on offender disclosing information	1	6	0	0
Based on Canadian model/culture	–	5	–	–
Items too difficult to assess – POs not qualified to assess	0	4	0	0
Information not always available for all items	0	1	0	0
Other problems with questions	9	7	4	0
Unspecified problems with areas/questions (specify areas and problem)	1	4	0	0
Burden to complete	17	9	2	0
Time-consuming – takes more or too much time	8	5	0	0
Adds to paperwork/another form to fill in/more bureaucracy	7	5	2	0
Lot of repetition within ACE system	6	–	–	–
Needs to fit in with computer system	5	0	0	0
Quarterly progress is too frequent	5	–	–	–
Too general/overkill for certain groups/could trigger other more specific assessments	3	0	0	0
Too many forms within ACE system	3	–	–	–
Forms within ACE don't fit together	2	–	–	–
Unfamiliarity means it takes more time	1	0	0	0
Should be in one document to make links	1	0	0	0
Offender burden for self-completion	1	–	–	–
Doesn't contribute to/help POs work	7	17	0	0
Focussed on ACE/LSI-R/CMI areas of assessment anyway	4	12	0	0
Doesn't feed into system or tell you what you're going to do	3	11	0	0
Limited as prisons not using	1	0	0	0
Impedes relationship with offender	1	0	0	0
Omissions/lack of detail in form	4	15	1	0
Misses out certain areas/factors that officer should ask	4	14	1	0
Needs more detailed/specific questions in certain areas	3	10	0	0
No room for offender viewpoint	1	4	0	0
Limitations of forms	12	12	4	4
Need officer opinions/Just gives you a score/number	3	8	0	4

Doesn't give a true picture of someone/questions are limited				
Forms/tick boxes inappropriate for work/	6	5	3	0
people don't fit into boxes	5	5	1	0
Not transparent/meaningful	4	1	0	4
Too rigid	4	0	0	0
Doesn't record progress very well	3	2	0	2
Depends on officers' knowledge of area	1	0	0	0
Notes/evidence boxes should be compulsory	1	–	–	–
Problems with concept/inclusion of items	4	11	0	0
Questions relevance of items to re-offending	4	7	0	0
Too many static factors	0	6	0	0
Problems with weighting of questions/factors	0	4	0	0
Certain factors all offenders score the same way on	0	3	0	0
Items overlap/measure same thing	0	2	0	0
Form not user-friendly	6	5	0	0
Form difficult to fill out	2	4	0	0
Don't like crossing out factors – circle instead	–	2	–	–
Other problems with design/layout	5	0	0	0
Cost of instrument	–	3	–	–
Not suitable for blanket use	0	1	0	0
Lack of training	1	0	0	0
Not validated by research	1	0	0	0
No feedback to officers	1	0	0	0
Timescale – have to complete circumstances at time of contact rather than offence	1	0	0	0
Encourages you to report on change where there often is none	0	0	0	1
Other	8	8	1	0

- the wording of the item "absence of recent participation in an organised activity" – "people look at you like you've gone berserk"; "an organised activity can be playing pool for people who are leading disorganised lives."

- the term "probation/parole" used in item 9.

- the wording used in the education items.

- the use of "inference" and "psychosis" in the mental health items.

Another problem with LSI-R, mentioned by nine officers, was that the language was too "Americanised" or was obviously from a different criminal justice system, for example, "institutional misconduct". Seven officers criticised its use of double-negatives in items 35 and 36. (One version of item 35 was: "Few anti-criminal acquaintances".) About a quarter (6) said it was problematic having to rely on offender information for certain items in LSI-R. Difficulties were cited with the section on education (qualifications, whether suspended or expelled), on criminal history and with marital/family relationships. Four POs felt they were not qualified to assess offenders' mental health in the emotional/personal section. The same number felt that the form was based on Canadian culture and some parts of the form were not appropriate to the UK (4). One officer wondered whether

> There's a difference in the sort of culture in Canada from here... And therefore they would give greater weighting to certain things than we would here. Obvious example is unemployment, I mean, there's no welfare state in Canada, so, or perhaps not as developed as here. So that unemployment in say Canada is perhaps a big, bigger problem and therefore greater predictor of crime, whereas here nearly everybody on probation is out of work and its almost like normal for the area almost.

Three officers felt that items or the coding scales in LSI-R were too subjective. One officer said this had led to problems in recording progress as *"they go up on the score and that's because you've scored it slightly differently that time around to what you did the time before."*

Thirteen officers who used ACE had problems in completing the forms. One of the main concerns expressed by six officers was that the forms were subjective, with five officers having concerns that the scoring used differed between occasions and officers: *"if I can't be consistent in my own scoring, then what hope is there for the rest of us to be consistent with each other?"* One officer also mentioned the impact this had on progress: *"if someone else had done a 3 initially... it's not clear [to me] what [was] going through their mind at the time and how they've assessed it, so it's difficult for me to know whether there's been movement or not".* Five officers said that the language used was sometimes ambiguous or unclear, particularly the self-completion element (3 officers).

Other problems included the omission of a date on review forms (2), repetition in the problem checklist (1) and difficulties in estimating the risk of re-offending (1). The four CMI users in this group were all talking about the same problem concerning the assessment of offenders' motivation. In the current version, offenders' overall motivation was assessed. Officers wanted to assess this with respect to each specific need/factor identified.

No officers using the Berkshire AF mentioned problems completing the form itself.

(ii)   Burden to complete

The most common complaint among ACE users was that the forms were in some way a burden to complete. All but one of the 18 officers interviewed mentioned one or more problems with this. Eight officers said that ACE took too much time to complete, or that they had insufficient time to complete it, for example, *"it's very time- consuming to just manage to get... all the information in this report. You've got to fill this out and then you actually think, oh gosh, wish we didn't have to do this."* Seven officers said it added to paperwork and bureaucracy even to the extent of *"so much paperwork is involved that it feels like it's impeding our work with offenders"*. Six said there was a lot of repetition within the ACE forms. One improvement, suggested by five officers, was to fit ACE in with current computing systems. The same number felt that filling forms out quarterly was too frequent, an *"over-kill... in paperwork"* and *"when little has changed... it becomes a paper exercise"*. Three officers said that there were too many forms to complete in ACE. Another problem, mentioned by three officers, was that questions were too general and covered too many groups. In a couple of cases, asking such general questions had caused problems, for example, with domestic violence: *"many people who have never been involved in domestic violence found that an offensive question. Why should you be asking me about domestic violence when I'm on probation for excess alcohol?"*

The issue of paperwork was also frequently raised by the LSI-R interviewees, even though not always directed towards LSI-R. Five officers said that LSI-R just added to paperwork and bureaucracy and was *"another form to fill in"*. The same number said that it created extra work and took more time to do, in a climate of increasing time constraints. Two officers using CMI also felt that it added paperwork and bureaucracy, given that *"we're bogged down with paper"*. (Because CMI had only just been piloted, officers in Kent were still filling in some duplicate forms in parallel, but this was to be rationalised in due course.) The concise nature of the Berkshire AF meant that no officers said it added to paperwork.

(iii)   Doesn't help or contribute to POs' work

There were two main complaints here: against ACE and LSI-R only. Over half (12) the officers using LSI-R in assessments felt that it did not tell them anything that they did not already know, that *"the information you get from an LSI-R you would have got anyway"*. Fewer (4) officers using ACE felt this way.

The other concern, mentioned by half the officers using LSI-R, was that it did not feed in to the current system: it did not aid officers in deciding what they were going to do with an offender, and the score had no meaning for them. There were suggestions that LSI-R should be better integrated within probation administration systems, and with CRAMS and supervision plans. Some officers felt extremely negative about the lack of interface: *"as long as when you write something down, you know what to do with it at the end. I mean it's all very well writing all this stuff down but if nothing happens with it, then it's useless."* Another felt that *"that form doesn't necessarily help us, or that system help us to do the job better. It's feeding another system which seems to be additional to the work that you are trying to do with the client."*

A smaller number (3) of officers using ACE agreed that it did not help them decide what they were going to do with offenders. One officer cited the example of an offender involved in domestic violence: *"it's a section that may identify for the sake of a computer that yes this person has problems but moving on from there, it doesn't tell you much. I know you've got notes to expand but I just feel as if it's not adequate in itself because I've also undertaken courses with a sex offenders' unit and I've covered issues of domestic violence, things like that, and I think their view probably would agree that that again isn't adequate, you know, there's got to be more behind it than just a simple coding of this that and the other".*

(iv)   Omissions/lack of detail in form

LSI-R was also criticised by 15 officers for missing out or lacking detail in certain areas. About two-thirds (14) of officers said that LSI-R missed out factors it should be asking about. Many of these were referring to concepts related to risk of harm. Five officers said LSI-R should contain questions about risk of harm. Also mentioned were the seriousness of offences (3), patterns and nature of offending (3), history of violent offending (3), frequency of offending (1), situational analysis of offending (1), self-harm (1) and likely victims (1). Two officers said LSI-R should collect information on cultural/environmental factors, and two said it should record how offenders presented themselves to the officer[6].

Just under half (10) the officers said some of the items on LSI-R lacked detail. Areas cited were education (2), leisure/recreation (1), family (1), domestic violence (1), violence (1), mental health (1), companions (1), finance (1), criminal history (2), drugs (1), employment

---

6   Other areas mentioned fpr LSI-R were: victim awareness, consequences of offending, responsibility, other agency involvement, literacy, other risk behaviours, for example, gambling, cognitive skills, responsivity, accommodation issues, support systems, pre-meditation, non-criminogenic needs, poverty, emotional needs and emotional damage.

(1) and attitudes (1). Four officers said there should be room for the offenders' viewpoint. Two officers said offenders should be able to identify their own needs or problems. Other examples of questions that could be asked were about their family (1), motivation for offending (1) and perceived risk of re-offending (1)

Omissions were not seen by as many officers using ACE or CMI to be a problem, or by any of the AF users. One CMI user said that it *"focuses on the here and now... rather than perhaps the past"*. Four officers using ACE thought that it missed out certain areas, two of whom said that it did not really ask about offenders' needs: *"I don't think this is concerned about the needs of the offender. It's very criminogenic which misses so much of an individual's life."* One officer said that ACE did not ask about race, gender and domestic violence and another about victims and harm caused. Three officers thought it lacked detail in certain areas, those mentioned being pre-convictions and own experience of being victimised (1), the supervision plans and reviews (1) and current offence (1)

(v)   Limitations of forms

Four out of the five users of CMI and AF, and about two-thirds of the officers using LSI-R and ACE (14 and 12 respectively) had concerns about limitations of the forms.

Three CMI users thought that the forms did not give a true picture of somebody, for example, *"there is actually other information that is necessary to get a sense of a person, and the tick box won't tell you, you know, everything about them."* Another officer felt that it was difficult to fit people into boxes: *"[offenders] are not automatons... they are human beings and... there are shades of issues, I suppose, shades of problems."*

Four of the Berkshire officers were concerned with the fact that the forms were coded and gave no space for officers to highlight any information. One officer felt that *"all you know is figures and ticks and crosses, you don't get no, sort of, feel for the offender."* They also felt that the document was not meaningful to others because of the limited information it could convey, and this caused a number of problems. Three officers said they could not show it to the offender, which meant that there was no document they could use to engage with them or agree the scope of the order. Four felt that it was not transparent to other officers, particularly important when a case was being transferred or temporarily supervised by another officer. One officer gave the example that *"you could get somebody on office duty and you can have a look there and I don't think it's going to tell me enough about this person... I'm perhaps looking at somebody who I might know drinks too much and hasn't got somewhere to live - that's about it - and I would like a bit more information when I'm trying to deal with somebody I don't know."*

Although the LSI-R form has a small space for notes and special circumstances, about a third (8) of officers thought that there should be more room for officers' opinions, for them to express their instincts or gut feelings about a case, and that LSI-R only provided a number. The information conveyed was felt to be limited: *"I'd rather see what an officer has to say than look at this. There's nothing really here"; "Perhaps I just want to know more than someone's score of 37."* Some officers did use the space provided on the forms: *"Sometimes when you are filling it in and you're thinking it would be helpful to put something else in, sometimes I just write things on the back sheet because I feel that I haven't had a chance to like put it anywhere else."*

Five thought that LSI-R did not give a true or full picture of an individual, for a variety of reasons, for example, *"it's all yes/no answers or degrees of"* and *"if you just ask them those questions [on the form] you miss out on quite a lot."* One officer commented that LSI-R could identify two different people as almost the same. Five had general reservations about the use of LSI-R for this type of work. One officer said *"the problem with it is that we are talking about people, and people do not fit into these boxes."* Two officers said that LSI-R was limited in how well it recorded progress of an offender (see Chapter 2).

A third (6) of ACE users also felt that the forms did not present a true picture of offenders, for example, *"when you're using words, I suppose they are more descriptive, you know you can sort of indicate in-betweens better than just using headings and numbers."* Five felt that such forms were not appropriate for work with offenders: *"it simplifies the people we are dealing with. I'm old fashioned enough to believe you just cannot fit people on to a form."* Four ACE users were concerned that the forms were not transparent, whether it be for the officer themselves reviewing the case, other officers looking at the case, the offender or other parties such as HMIP inspectors. The same number felt that the forms were too rigid. Concern was also expressed (by 3 officers) that ACE did not record progress very well: *"the quarterly reviews... don't really encourage any kind of explanations of what is going on other than in the very broad terms of, you know, achievement of objectives or what have you, partial achievements, and setting new ones.."* Three officers thought ACE just gave a score and nothing else.

(vi)   Problems with concept and inclusion of certain items

Half the officers using LSI-R (11) had concerns about the concept or inclusion of certain items in the form. About a third (7) questioned the relevance of certain items to re-offending. Examples given were: leisure/recreation, particularly the item "could make better use of time" (3), education (1), being unemployed (1), living in a high crime area (1) and whether someone had two or three convictions (1). Six officers said that there were too many static factors included in the form, which *"you can't do anything about"*. This led to other problems, for example, *"we don't have any control over lots of these factors, accommodation. And so to use [LSI-R] as a measure of effectiveness is difficult."* Four officers had concerns about the weighting of certain questions and factors, with two thinking that education and employment were weighted too heavily in the form. Three officers said that certain items were answered in the same way by all or most offenders, for example, being unemployed. Two officers saw overlap between certain factors, one between the mental health and drugs/alcohol questions, and one within the emotional/personal section. This was not seen to be a problem by any CMI or AF users and only by a few ACE officers. Only four officers questioned the relevance of items in the form. Areas cited were sexuality (2 officers), sexual behaviour (1), family/personal relationships (1) and being in care (1).

(vii)   Form is not user-friendly

Five officers using LSI-R thought that the form was not user-friendly in some way, with three saying it was difficult to fill out. Five ACE-using officers also had problems with the design of the form. Specific improvements were: giving more space for recording contacts, putting both client and officer opinions onto one form, improving the layout of the self-completion questionnaire and supervision plans and reducing the amount of space given in the initial assessment form (although more officers liked having the space available to write notes or evidence). None of the CMI or AF users said the form was not user-friendly.

(viii)   Other problems

One in seven officers (3) using LSI-R commented on the cost of the instrument. (LSI-R reportedly cost between 95p and £1.50 a form for probation services to use it.) One officer using LSI-R thought that it was not suitable for blanket use, and that POs should be able to select who they used it for. Another officer using AF said it encouraged officers to report change when often there was no reason for change. Other complaints about ACE (cited by one officer each) were a lack of training to complete it, the fact it was not validated by research, a lack of feedback about the information in the form to officers and problems caused by having to complete it about circumstances at the time of contact rather than at the time of the offence.

Effect on time of assessments

Officers were also asked whether assessments using the instruments took more or less time to complete than without them (Table 4.3). Just under half the ACE and LSI-R users said that there was no difference, particularly once officers had got used to the instruments. All of the Berkshire users said that assessments made with the AF were quicker. However, about half the ACE, LSI-R and CMI users said that assessments now took longer. Officers were also asked how much time it added per assessment. The average length of time added for the 11 LSI-R users who said it took longer was 18 minutes. Only five of the eight ACE users who said it took longer were able to estimate how much it added: on average, they said it added about 25 minutes.

Table 4.3 Effect on time to complete assessments: PO sample

	ACE	LSI-R	CMI	AF
More time	8	11	3	0
No difference	6	9	0	0
Less time	1	0	2	5
Only ever done assessments with instrument	1	1	0	0
Can't say	2	0	0	0
Total in sample	18	22	5	5

Usefulness in different aspects of work

Officers were asked to rate how useful they found the instruments in different areas of their work. Table 4.4 shows the number of officers who found the instruments useful and those who did not find them useful. (Other responses such as "don't know" are excluded from the table.) Overall, most ACE, AF and LSI-R officers found the instruments useful in their work, although four ACE and nine LSI-R users said they were not useful. Only two of the Kent officers felt that they had enough experience to rate its use overall: they both found it useful.

All of the instruments were rated by most users as useful at the PSR and/or supervision planning stages and in prioritising problems to be addressed, although six LSI-R and seven

ACE users said it was not useful for this. LSI-R had the most detractors at the PSR stage, with 6 officers saying it was not useful then. In terms of measuring progress, ACE was seen as useful by most officers, but opinion was divided on LSI-R and the AF, while only 2 officers using CMI said it was useful for this.

CMI was seen as useful to measure risk of re-offending by all the officers interviewed, while LSI-R was rated useful for this by 12 (as opposed to 5) officers. However, most of the ACE officers said ACE (and OGRS) was not useful for this, while the Berkshire officers were split 50:50. However, most AF users said their risk of harm assessment was useful, while only 2 CMI users felt able to say this. The ACE harm of assessment received mixed reviews, with similar numbers finding it useful and not useful.

None of the instruments performed particularly well on case recording: most ACE and AF users said their forms were not useful for this, as did about half the CMI users, and a slight minority of LSI-R users.

Table 4.4 Usefulness of instruments: PO sample

	ACE	LSI-R	CMI	AF
Measuring risk of re-offending:				
Very/fairly useful	3	12	5	2
Not very/not at all useful	8	5	0	2
Prioritising problems to be addressed:				
Very/fairly useful	11	13	5	4
Not very/not at all useful	7	6	0	0
Case recording:				
Very/fairly useful	9	6	2	1
Not very/not at all useful	8	8	2	4
Overall work with offenders:				
Very/fairly useful	14	12	2	3
Not very/not at all useful	4	9	0	0
Total in sample	18	22	5	5

5   Using the instruments: the manager's perspective

This chapter looks at how the SPOs interviewed used the instruments for management purposes, and the benefits and problems they had experienced.

Use of the instrument at management level tended to lag behind introduction at the practitioner level. Therefore, of the nine SPOs who managed staff using LSI-R, the eight SPOs who managed staff using ACE and two SPOs each from Kent and Berkshire, most either did not use or had only limited experience of using the instruments for management purposes.

Using the forms in middle management

(i)   LSI-R

There were four broad functions for which SPOs either used LSI-R or saw it as having potential:

- Allocation and targetting of resources. Five SPOs mentioned this, although only three of them were currently using it for this. LSI-R was felt to have strong potential here, because of its power in quantifying risk (in terms of re-offending): *"we're the first to have our own database from it which is giving us some fabulous results in terms of offender profiles, so we know where to target our resources."* Another SPO commented that *"it assists in the resource allocation and I think that's the bit that might actually have more of an impact in terms of quality and by that I mean quality of response to risk, rather than the quality of the assessment."* However, the point was also made that reliance on LSI-R alone was not possible as *"it doesn't necessarily address risk of dangerousness, which is the other missing factor."*

- Provision of information. Four officers said LSI-R was potentially useful for getting summary information on their team caseloads. Three had actually used LSI-R for this purpose, for example to get offender profiles of risks or needs. This was linked to use in allocation and targeting of resources, but could also be for other purposes, for example, *"I did do a small collation myself for a specific drug project and it was useful to be able to say the proportion of offenders who we knew to have major drug problems."*

- Monitoring officers' work. Although only one officer was actively using it, LSI-R was seen by three officers as having a role to play in supervising certain (though not all) aspects of individual officers' work. Areas mentioned were checking that officers were addressing appropriate needs for supervision (2 responses), checking assessments (1) and checking referrals (1). However, LSI-R was seen as one of several tools to use in monitoring officers' work, rather than being used by itself: "You wouldn't just rely on one piece of paper to check performance anyway, it would be part of a process... reading records, reading reports, supervision, observation: they're all part of the parcel of checking out officer performance."

- Two other officers felt that LSI-R had limited value in ensuring the quality of their teams' work, for example, "I think that [it] will be difficult to actually give a quality control of the assessment. They're all filled in so yes it happens... but whether or not to check whether it's filled in in the right way we would have to actually sit on people and actually watch them doing it and when they're doing it."

- Demonstrating effectiveness and looking at outcomes. Two officers saw potential in this, although neither was currently using LSI-R in this way. One SPO commented that "I think it's quite useful to think that we have some information that provides us with knowledge that we've done a good job really, using it at the beginning and the end and show some change."

One problem was reported by three SPOs, that of ensuring that forms are being filled out correctly. Two SPOs reported problems in how consistently forms were scored, and in the counting and addition of scores. Another problem was "it is very, very easy to stick a cross on the wrong yes or no answer, then come up with a very wrong scoring." The same officer emphasised how "how they are using the form, how they are scoring needs constant monitoring, because I think you get slippage, people get complacent about ticking boxes and scoring." Another SPO had had problems initially with officers missing questions. One SPO also said there was "too much use of the professional over-ride".

(ii)   ACE

SPOs who managed staff using ACE commented on three main areas, two of which overlapped with the LSI-R sample.

- Monitoring officers' work. Six SPOs said that ACE could be used in different aspects of monitoring their staff's work. The main role was in looking at what work officers were doing with offenders (4 responses), for example, "what [staff] are doing and what they're not doing" and "very clear checks that officers are actually conducting work that is associated with that assessment of needs". One SPO found the case recording role of ACE helped in this respect "because I can know exactly what's going on in any case at any time". Two SPOs (from the same service) also said that ACE could be used to check whether officers were making, or not making, appropriate referrals to, for example, groupwork programmes and accommodation and financial advice. Another SPO used it to check the PSR report.

- Again, there were seen to be limitations with how far ACE helped managers to supervise work. In checking referrals, for example, one officer commented that "there's nothing in itself that says 'ah, this is a need and this can be dealt with by... '". Another SPO felt that ACE focused on outcomes rather than processes, so that it was not helpful in diagnosing why problems in supervision were happening; they emphasised the need for space to comment on such problems. Two SPOs had experienced problems with monitoring work done by officers, because of problems with consistency. This also undermined the role of ACE in monitoring assessments: two SPOs cited problems with this: "we can look at consistency of assessments within an individual officer's caseload, I think we haven't yet looked at across officers how reliable that is." Another SPO thought that ACE "ensures that people are covering the same areas in their assessments, but I suppose you know there are other things that determine quality as well, but I mean, I think they probably help to improve the quality." Another commented that ACE "doesn't necessarily show how the assessment has been achieved".

- Provision of information. ACE was seen as having potential in providing information in a variety of ways, to managers (3) and also to officers (1) or in appraisals (1). Areas mentioned were demonstrating trends, needs, methods used and offender profiles. However, three officers said that at the time of survey, feedback systems had not yet been fully developed. One officer said that ACE as it stood did not provide adequate information about risk assessment.

- Allocation of cases. Three SPOs said ACE could have uses here, although only one had used it much in this way, as cases with higher ACE scores generally received more intensive supervision.

(iii) AF

The AF was currently being used in some aspects of management by both SPOs interviewed:

- Monitoring officers' work. The AF was used by both SPOs interviewed to monitor certain aspects of their officers' work. One SPO said it could be used to check how officers were using resources *"say accommodation and employment"*, including looking at referrals, for example, *"if an outcome is to help the person get into employment you can be looking at whether referrals are made to the employment services officer."* The other said it had a role in monitoring enforcement: *"I can see from the assessment framework that in terms of enforcement what's happened: you know, has the offender failed to make contact, if so has the officer you know taken breach action and if not, why not."*

- Allocation of cases. One SPO thought the AF had a role in allocation: *"I actually use the assessment framework to say, you know, who's got a proportion of caseload that is particularly risky... which is better than previously, where I might have a list of names and numbers in terms of caseload."*

The brevity of the document was seen as both an advantage and disadvantage. While both officers felt that *"I can just refer to one document instead of having to flick through the file to find the information"*, it was also recognised that the framework could not be used by itself to look at officers' work *"I would have to rely on talking to officers in supervision and that sort of thing."*

(iv) CMI

As the CMI had been only recently introduced, it was not yet being used fully for management purposes. However, it was envisaged that it might have use in:

- Monitoring officers' work. Two examples were given. One was looking at supervision activities and referrals, for example, *"finding out that the team are targeting probation orders correctly, that they are using partnership agencies to maximum effect, to support case management, that needs assessment is matching the kind of levels of risk as identified by the CMI".* The other SPO thought that it could be used to see how officers were spending their time and using other resources, by *"provid[ing] a very good at-a-glance look at whether a probation officer is devoting their time appropriately to criminogenic activities".*

- Targeting reporting schemes appropriately. One SPO thought that the CMI could eventually be used to look at groups referred to the (lower risk) reporting schemes operating in Kent. It could be useful both in moving low-risk offenders more quickly to less intensive supervision, and in checking that only those with low risk go onto such schemes.

However, as with the other instruments, it was felt that there were some limitations in using it to monitor assessment quality: *"it's a fallacy to assume that anything will guarantee consistency because people can always interpret things... I don't believe any particular paper instrument is going to say whether someone's made a quality assessment in the sense that you can't tell whether they filled in the right boxes just by looking at a piece of paper";* *"it still comes down to... the professionalism of the officer."*

Usefulness

SPOs were asked to rate how useful they found the instruments their staff were using in terms of management tasks. Table 5.1 shows the responses. The CMI had not been used extensively by middle managers. LSI-R was rated by most managers as useful (or potentially useful) in ensuring consistency in assessments: seven officers said it was useful here. Four SPOs said it could be useful in monitoring the quality of supervision and in providing management information. Half of the SPOs managing ACE staff said that ACE had use in ensuring the consistency of assessments, in monitoring the quality of assessments and supervision, in managing caseloads and in providing management information. Both Berkshire SPOs thought the AF was useful in ensuring consistency of assessments, but not useful in monitoring the quality. They were split on its use for managing caseloads.

Table 5.1 Usefulness of instruments in management: SPO sample

	ACE	LSI-R	CMI	AF
Ensuring consistency in assessments:				
Very/fairly useful	4	7	0	2
Not very/not at all useful	2	1	0	0
Monitoring quality of assessments:				
Very/fairly useful	4	3	1	0
Not very/not at all useful	1	1	0	2
Monitoring quality of supervision:				
Very/fairly useful	4	4	1	0
Not very/not at all useful	2	1	0	1
Monitoring other aspects:				
Very/fairly useful	2	1	1	1
Not very/not at all useful	2	2	0	0
Managing caseloads:				
Very/fairly useful	4	3	0	1
Not very/not at all useful	0	1	1	1
Management information:				
Very/fairly useful	4	4	1	1
Not very/not at all useful	0	0	0	0
Total in sample	8	9	2	2

6   Use of alternative and supplementary instruments

This chapter examines three different topics. First it looks at how suitable the existing instruments were for all groups of offenders and alternative methods suggested for looking at risk of re-offending and needs. It also looks at other tools used in addition to the four instruments. Lastly, it covers some comments made by POs and SPOs about links with prison assessments.

Suitability for all groups and alternative methods used

About half (10 out of 18) the ACE officers said that ACE was not suitable for all types of offenders (Table 6.1). The most common groups mentioned were motoring offenders, primarily drunk drivers (4 officers), offenders with no real 'problems' or where the offence appeared trivial (3), women (3), sexual offenders (3) and lifers (3). Other groups mentioned were ethnic minorities (2) and unco-operative offenders (2).

A larger number of LSI-R users (17 out of 22) said that LSI-R was not suitable for all groups. Fifteen officers mentioned its unsuitability for sex offenders, six for juveniles (16 and 17 year olds), and six for motoring offenders (again primarily drunk drivers). The inappropriateness for sex offenders and juveniles more often seemed to reflect information officers had received in the training about the limitations of LSI-R for these groups rather than direct experience of its unsuitability for these groups. Other groups mentioned were domestic violence cases (4), women (3) and older people (3). Two officers also said it was unsuitable where the offence was very trivial.

Only one AF user felt it was not suitable for all offenders, commenting that it was *"difficult with a person who lacks any form of comprehension"*.

Two officers using CMI thought it was unsuitable for all groups. One officer specified domestic violence and sexual offenders, while the other cited mentally disordered offenders, those with learning difficulties, women, ethnic minorities and homosexual offenders.

Officers were asked to suggest alternative methods for assessing risk and need for the groups listed above, although in many cases no suggestions were made:

    i)   Sex offenders. It was suggested that assessment tools such as ACE and LSI-R were not suitable because *"sex offenders are a group of their own"*. Officers described them as *"devious"*, *"manipulative"* and *"good liars"*. Two officers thought that there was no type of structured assessment form which could be used effectively with them. Other recommended strategies included using intuition (1) and more detailed questioning (1). One officer also suggested that it might be more helpful to look at patterns, nature and type of offence, and risk of harm rather than risk of re-offending *"because with sex offenders you are actually making an assumption that if they've done it once they've probably done it again in the past."* One officer also made the point that sexual issues could be important even when the index offence was not a sexual one (the same point was also made about domestic violence).

Table 6.1 Suitability of instrument for all groups: PO sample

	ACE	LSI-R	CMI	AF
Suitable for all groups:				
Yes	8	5	2	1
No	10	17	3	4
Unsuitable for:				
Sex offenders	3	15	1	0
Juveniles	1	6	0	0
Motoring offenders	4	6	0	0
Domestic violence	1	4	1	0
Women	3	3	1	0
No problems/trivial offence	3	2	0	0
Lifers	3	1	0	0
Older people	1	3	0	0
Unco-operative/concealing	2	1	0	0
Ethnic minorities	2	0	1	0
Mentally disordered	1	1	1	0
Middle class/white collar	1	1	0	0
One-off offences	1	1	0	0
Drug users	0	1	0	0
Alcohol users	1	0	0	0
First-time offenders	1	0	0	0
Learning difficulties	1	0	1	0
Dangerous offenders	0	1	0	0
Other	1	1	1	1
Total	18	22	5	5

ii)   Juveniles. In working with juveniles, it was suggested that LSI-R should look more closely at education and family support (1), outside school activities (1), and family relationships (1). Versions of ACE and LSI-R suitable for young offenders are currently being developed.

iii) Motoring offenders, primarily drunk drivers. Officers working with both ACE and LSI-R identified similar problems with current assessment arrangements for such offenders. Drink-drivers in particular tended to score very low on the assessment, or came out as having a very low risk of re-offending. This was most often attributed to the fact that they had relatively stable lifestyles (5) were generally well-educated (2), in stable employment (4) and with few money worries (2). They were also described as being mostly in secure marital/family relationships (2), and having stable accommodation (2). According to two officers using LSI-R, the assessment looked at *"environmental and historical factors"* such as the above but did not really pick up on emotional, attitudinal and personal factors. (Three officers believed these to have a high profile in such offending behaviour.) It was suggested that assessments for this type of offender should concentrate more on anti-social attitudes (2), responsibility attitudes to road safety (2), and the history or patterns of previous offending (2).

iv)   Domestic violence. There was little comment on possible alternatives for assessing domestic violence cases. One LSI-R user suggested that *"there could be a section focusing on their views... how you treat people within relationships perhaps, or what did they expect from relationships, those sort of questions."*

v)   Women. LSI-R users thought the different issues which should be looked at more closely when working with women offenders were financial matters (2), family (2), relationships (2) and the fact that most women choose not to or are unable to work (1). Suggestions for better assessment included *"looking more closely at the history of their offending and then the consequences of it... for them"* and providing better social assistance (2). Two officers working with ACE generally believed that *"the forms need to be developed further, as offending in this group relates to different types of issues,"* although they did not specify these in detail.

vi) No problems/trivial offences. For trivial offences such as shoplifting, one officer felt *"it seems an awful lot to go through"* especially if there are very few needs to be addressed. Another officer believed that *"if they don't have real needs or 'problems', its irrelevant to try and look for them."* Other officers thought that in these circumstances, an assessment should concentrate more on the offence itself (1), the attitudes of the offender (2) and the patterns of previous behaviour (2).

Supplementary tools in use

Only a few officers (three in the ACE and LSI-R samples apiece and two in the local instrument sample) said they used additional tools. Three LSI-R users and one Berkshire officer mentioned the use of OGRS. Eleven ACE users also mentioned using OGRS in conjunction with ACE (even though all officers should use it as part of the ACE forms). In all, 11 officers had some scepticism about OGRS' performance. The main complaint against it, made by seven officers, was that it gave questionable results for individual offenders, particularly for domestic violence cases, sex offenders, women offenders, or for those with adult prison sentences. One officer said the score was meaningless, two that they were unsure about its validity and another that *"whoever invented that needs to be shot, it's a waste of breath"*. Seven officers thought that OGRS was useful in some way: Three officers used it with offenders and two said that the forms were easier in some way. Two officers saw it as a *"basic guide"* or *"rough tool"*. Another thought: *"I can use it any number of times... it's quite neat and it's statistical which I think makes it attractive."* Other instruments mentioned (by one officer each) were referral forms for programmes, alcohol dependency questionnaires, seriousness scores and stages of change motivation assessments.

Links with prison assessments

Fourteen POs and SPOs (four in the ACE, seven in the LSI-R and three in the locally developed instrument sample) made comments about the links between probation and prison risk assessments, even though they were not specifically asked about this.

Eight officers (six in the LSI-R and two in the ACE sample) thought the present situation could be improved by making assessment procedures consistent between prisons and probation. Officers experienced various difficulties:

- Five officers mentioned problems caused by inconsistencies between each system's risk assessment procedures, for example, *"I've thought from the beginning what the Home Office really should be doing is looking at developing a risk system that covers both aspects, not just re-offending but also risk of harm and having that consistent across all services including the prison as well. Because everyone's is completely different, even if it's based on similar research, then the lay-out, the language, the terminology is very different."* [LSI-R SPO] One ACE PO saw the solution as: *"If they [prisons] use the ACE document then we would be speaking... the same language and they would have that as soon as the punter went [down. The] PSR would follow the punter when he was sent down [and] the ACE document."* [ACE PO]

- Two officers said there was duplication between prison and probation procedures. An LSI-R PO described their current work: *"I have to fill in the information form which actually goes back to the prison which feeds into the process of doing their sentence planning. Which again is a risk assessment system. So they are asking us again for similar things to what we've already done here [on LSI-R]. ... So a lot of similar questions go towards a different set of forms to get to a similar point really."* One ACE SPO said: *"At the moment we are duplicating, prisons are doing their own assessment, we've already done [ACE]. We ought to be making better use of what's already been done and... we could actually incorporate the criminogenic needs from this [ACE] assessment in terms of the sentence management."*

- Two officers said there was inconsistency within the prison system, exacerbated by the number of prisons each service had to deal with. One LSI-R SPO described the situation as: *"extremely inconsistent up and down the country... my team deals with 45 different prisons, so the propensity for inconsistency is huge."*

- Another problem with throughcare cases (mentioned by 2 officers) which impacted on risk assessment was that officers often did not deal with offenders in custody due to time and financial pressures, for example, *"at the moment I'm not very good at throughcare. I'll put my hand up to that. People go to prison and they go away as far as I'm concerned and I can get on with stuff that's in my face which is a terrible attitude to have but it helps me to survive."*

- One officer said that the current prison risk predictor *"is basically an actuarial one and so flawed because it could have been one offence in the past, could have been murder, but it would come out as low risk, because it doesn't allow for professional over-ride"*.

Two officers said that the tool used at PSR stage for offenders in custody and subsequently released on license had been valuable: *"to have issues that were identified at the LSI-R stage being dealt with in the prison and then on release [to] say: well, is there a difference here?"*

The Kent CMI which was completed at the start of supervision was also seen as helpful here for *"people who don't have a PSR then serve a prison sentence [because] often none of the other risk assessments are done that would normally be done at PSR stage so these guys just can end up coming out of prison and there's a hastily written supervision plan."*

One officer had used LSI-R with someone in prison because *"there was no baseline to assess his risk so he couldn't see whether he'd improved or not, so I employed it with him because I thought there needs to be a starting point for this man."*

One ACE user had found the instrument useful in work with someone on license, in *"using [sections of ACE] in conjunction with enhanced thinking courses [that] person went through at college in prison and [I] combined the two to see if that's kind of useful information...[it] acts like a working document which I can then refer to later on to see if there's any movement"*. Another officer, talking about the Kent CMI, thought there was potential in using an adapted version of the instrument (mainly the case management element) in prison: *"There was a particular prison at one time which used to produce something like this... for each prisoner. It was a very crude list of factors on a T-card and the idea was that when the personal officer... had a few moments to spare, he would pull somebody's T-card out and it would say drink problems', so he would go off and have a discussion with someone about their drink problems and get them to complete a drink diary whatever and then he would write you know, whether it had been done or needed more work on it and then the T-card would go back in the office index. ... I could imagine the prison using this in a not dissimilar way to trigger personal officers."*

However, one officer foresaw problems with having one instrument for both services because *"there's a different emphasis in our areas of work... prisons will have... to be assessing far more serious... offenders... whereas we will have a much wider mix and quite often at the PSR stage, you know, you're dealing with everybody"*. This officer and another also foresaw more general difficulties with a national risk assessment as *"someone who will be classified as high risk of harm in this district is not the same person who in Merseyside will be classified as high risk of harm very distinct differences."*

Assessing the risk of harm

This chapter looks at the way that instruments covered in the study dealt with or linked in with the assessment of risk of harm and dangerousness (as opposed to re-offending or re-conviction).

LSI-R

The LSI-R form is not designed to cover risk of harm at all, it looks only at the risk of re-offending. Officers using LSI-R were asked about the procedures in their service to assess risk of harm and dangerousness. Three of the services, Northumbria, Durham and Teeside, used risk of harm assessments based on models developed by Brearley (see Brearley, 1982). (One officer in Durham also mentioned using checklists based on Hazel Kemshall's work (see Kemshall, 1996)). Officers in West Glamorgan completed a risk assessment on all offenders at the PSR stage. Surrey was piloting a system called RAMAS for higher risk offenders (those considered dangerous for a variety of reasons, including a high score (37 or more) on LSI-R), which some officers had been trained to use.[7]

About half (12 out of 22) the officers using LSI-R saw the lack of harm assessment as a limitation of the instrument, for example *"if the offending behaviour [an offender] exhibit[s] is harmful offending behaviour, obviously that gives you an indication that they are likely to repeat harmful behaviour. But it kind of stops there I think really"*. Another problem in relation to this was that *"we are getting some real strange scores on people that are very dangerous and risky"*. Harm was seen as more important to determine than the risk of re-offending for a variety of reasons. In one service, the LSI-R score was being used to identify high-risk offenders for a particular programme which was causing problems with the type of offenders being referred (2 officers): *"most people feel that 'high risk' should mean high risk of harm, then this follows that [LSI-R] is not a very good predictor of that."* Another officer pointed out that when looking at prioritising resources and time, officers had to focus on dangerous people rather than people with a high risk of re-offending. This was backed up

---

7 RAMAS stands for Risk Assessment, Management and Audit System. It is designed to address dangerousness, mental instability, self harm/suicide risk and vulnerability. The risk assessment element of the system is a four-page form which includes an extensive risk checklist which includes factors such as history of aggression/violence, emotional control problem, impulsive, recent hospital admissions. Officers must indicate whether these factors are absent or present, or if information is unknown, along with comments. The form also includes needs and skills (resources) assessments, risk parameters, other agencies involved. There is an emphasis on inter-agency networking.

by four of the SPOs interviewed, who said they focussed on harm rather than re-offending as the criteria in allocating cases and deciding levels of supervision, prioritising officer time and resources, supervising officers and in making defensible decisions. As one SPO put it, *"I've got hundreds of people at risk of re-offending here because of the scale of the drugs problem. Not everybody's dangerous."*

Five POs wanted forms to include both risk of re-offending and harm, and four officers thought that certain questions on LSI-R could be expanded to cover harm. The areas to be expanded to achieve this were: nature and type of previous offences (5), violent/sexual offending (e.g. degree of violence, history of violence) (5), patterns and frequency of offending (4), seriousness of offences (2), identity of victims (1) and child protection (1). Two SPOs also thought that there might be scope for amalgamating risk of harm and risk of re-offending assessments, although one officer said, *"I suspect it may become a very complicated form"*. However, two POs said that the two types of assessment were incompatible, and in particular did not want risk of harm to be reduced to an LSI-R type format because *"it's individual factors about that person so it's not just a tick box or a cross"*. One officer thought that their existing systems (LSI-R and RAMAS) *"complement each other nicely"*. Another officer commented about LSI-R and RAMAS that *"[LSI-R] gives you just a sort of flat historical view whereas... [RAMAS]... is a living view."* One officer felt that *"you [don't] need more than one tool, I think you should have one or the other. How many tools do we need really to tell us that somebody's going to re-offend?"*

Although most officers seemed clear about the distinction between risk of harm and re-offending, 3 officers commented that there was or had been confusion between the two: *"Sometimes it's quite hard to divorce in your mind, you know, that you are talking about risk of harm and not risk of re-offending because sometimes you know they're tied in together and you've got to remind yourself all the time when you are doing this that what you are looking at is, you know, the risk of harm"*. One officer thought that LSI-R had helped to clarify the difference between the two: *"Most people had a great difficulty separating the risk of re-offending from risk of dangerousness when we started on this process, that, kind of, people got the two mixed up in a sense and we talk about one when they meant the other. And I suppose having the LSI-R and the risk [of harm] paperwork has enabled us to separate the two that can be two different things in a sense. That someone can be high risk of re-offending but not if they are shoplifter, then there's not particularly a high risk of dangerousness. But in other cases it can be both depending on the type of offence."* Two SPOs interviewed also said that the introduction of LSI-R had helped in this respect.

ACE

The ACE assessment includes a short section on risk of harm and dangerousness, which asks whether the offender presents a risk to children; the public; staff or other service users; and themselves. In West Midlands, the ACE assessment constituted the main risk of harm assessment, and officers also listed the factors likely to increase or decrease the degree of harm on the ACE forms. In Warwickshire, managers carried out an initial risk assessment, under a set of concurrent procedures based on static factors, upon allocation of the PSR. The ACE assessment (dynamic factors) is then taken into account at the start of an order when deciding on registration. POs using ACE were asked what they thought of the ACE risk of harm questions. Hereford and Worcester, by contrast, has concurrent procedures by which officers assess risk of harm. This is part of an overall Management of Risk (MOR) policy, where officers complete assessments on all offenders, covering: the likely risk behaviour, potential damage/harm, timing, circumstances and likely victims of harmful behaviour, agency involvement, contact with children and safeguards. High-risk offenders were placed on a register. In Northumbria, officers completed a risk assessment on all offenders adapted from Brearley, which asks them to consider predisposing hazards, situational hazards, strengths and dangers. In Warwickshire, managers carried out a risk assessment based on static factors before the PSR was completed.

In terms of usefulness, two out of 18 officers said that the ACE risk of harm assessment was "very useful", and seven that it was "fairly useful". Six officers found it "not very useful", and two "not useful at all". All but one of those who found it useful came from Warwickshire or Northumbria. Three officers (from Hereford and Worcester) said that the ACE harm assessment was only a reflection or summary of the concurrent risk of harm assessment: they did not regard it as an assessment in its own right. Two officers in another service said they had too many risk assessment forms to complete: *"I think I've mentioned six different risks forms or ways of assessing, which go on six different documents."*

POs mentioned some positive features of the ACE risk of harm questions. Two officers said it helped focus the officers' thinking: *"it makes me work out what bothers me about a case"*; *"it makes me really focus my attention on a precise nature of concerns if I have them."* Two other officers thought it helped them be more thorough in risk of harm assessments. One officer felt it could act as a trigger to *"alert you to risk and who was at risk"*. Another thought it potentially enhanced the other risk of harm assessment by acting as a double-check and picking up factors that might have been missed in one assessment. One officer felt that using the form made questions easier to ask.

Two POs thought that ACE gave a more standard definition of risk of harm, for example, *"everyone's view of risk was different but now with the standard questions I think it's a lot more clearer"*; *"risk for me is such an umbrella term these days, it could mean anything to anybody, so at least there is a risk of re-offending separated from a risk of harm separated from a risk of something else, so that is better for me."* However, of some concern was the confusion about the role of the risk of harm assessment showed by two officers:

- *"The risk factor that we're looking at is risk of re-offending... when I'm looking at risk assessment in my head, that's what I'm thinking of. So when they actually come in to this section of risk of harm to children, to others... the majority of people we come across it is totally inapplicable, you fix somebody up for driving whilst disqualified, what relevance has it got? Well you could say I suppose it's risk [to] a child - if they're driving whilst disqualified, the child is run over... but it seems that risk of harm to me doesn't actually say anything that is specifically tied in to what we're supposed to be about which is reducing offending. ... I would say that would be the major area to me - it's confusion because we had a training day on risk assessment which was to do with presented risk of re-offending and then we got that dropped on us which was about whether somebody was a risky person in terms of offending against children, getting involved in punch ups or whatever and the two don't go together".*

- *"The risk assessment section, it's a very weak section, I always cross out the degree of harm wording and actually put list the factors likely to increase the risk of re-offending or risk to the public".*

In terms of limitations of the risk of harm assessment, four officers felt ACE was too basic and unspecific, with one giving the following example: *"Say for instance you've got risk of harm to children, again it's just a simple numbering, you know, of 0-3 and if I had concerns in that particular area, I would certainly be asking more questions than whether I had, you know, identified problems up to serious concern. I'd expect you to know all sorts of other things to identify exactly what the risks were, who's at risk."* Another officer felt that the questions were too blunt, e.g. risk to children. Two officers had experienced problems where they felt the questions were inappropriate to certain offenders, for example, *"if you talk to a driving while disqualified individual and excess alcohol... they don't see themselves in these [risk of harm] categories, so it alienates to a certain degree."*

One officer suggested there should more questions on *"effects on others plus victims"* if ACE was to cover risk of harm sufficiently. One of the SPOs interviewed also thought the ACE harm assessment could be improved by including the *"historical or pre-existing factors and the situational factors and whatever which inform a decision about level of risk."* Another problem had been found with using the form for Schedule 1 offenders: *"kicking off with risk to children... leads them into believing this is some sort of Schedule 1 risk assessment... so therefore thereafter their responses are very different, they've been led."* One PO felt that *"it would be nice if there was somewhere [ACE] could tie in with risk assessments, you know, public protection risks."* Another thought that the Brearley assessment could be developed to fit into the ACE forms.

CMI

The Kent CMI includes a section listing 24 factors related to dangerousness and harm. For each factor specified, officers indicate the focus of behaviour as either towards the offender themselves (self-harm), staff, children, the public, specific individuals or other. The CMI stands in contrast to the other instruments in being *"the only document now for assessing potential harm or dangerousness in Kent... and this is the one which is tied into Kent's Public Protection Index."* Two officers said they found the CMI harm assessment "very useful" and two found it "fairly useful".

Four of the five officers interviewed found the structure of the different factors helpful in assessing risk of harm and dangerousness, in making them focus on all the different aspects of harm and to be more thorough. Two officers said that it had been useful in clarifying the distinction between risk of harm and re-offending. This was also mentioned by one of the SPOs: *"I think that what this has actually clarified is that risk and harm and dangerousness is different from predicted risk of re-offending in terms of an actual risk assessment. So for that degree, although it caused some confusion, it is now, I think, distilled in people's mind what the difference between those two elements of risk and need are, which has been for the good really."*

One officer found the focus of behaviour categorisation useful, the fact that it *"would complement sort of gut feelings I've had about people"* and clarify thinking in terms of work to be done with offenders. Another officer found advantages in that *"it gives a good quick analysis of the dangerous harm of that individual"*, which could be backed up by additional notes as necessary. One SPO also commented that *"it offers potentially a sort of at-a-glance indication of what the risks are and where they are."*

One officer was less enthusiastic about it and found some problems with filling out the focus of behaviour: *"they don't quite fit comfortably into this sort of tick box mode"*, although they liked the patterns of behaviour listed. They also thought that *"it's too busy, with too much information on it... it needs to tell you quickly is this person serious risk or not and it doesn't really tell you that."* Another officer mentioned the general limitation that *"with things like risk of harm and dangerousness... it would be quite dangerous to rely completely on CMI or any kind of tick box thing"*, particularly as *"it doesn't look at patterns... and I think that, you know, that kind of assessment you're never going to get it on a form. You know that, that has to be some sort of written assessment"*. One of the SPOs interviewed agreed that identification of a harm factor on the form was only the first step to assessing an offender's potential dangerousness.

AF

On the Berkshire AF (see above), officers have to indicate whether offenders present a significant risk of dangerous behaviour, either to the public, staff or self, after consideration of a number of factors, grouped into antecedents, behaviour and conditions. In addition, as one SPO described it, *"assessing risk is obviously part of the assessment framework. But... the way of assessing risk would be determined through a variety of means, obviously using one of Hazel Kemshall's models and discussion... between the manager and case manager."* The other commented that *"certainly in my team we are using [the AF] in conjunction with other things."*

Officers also complete additional forms to the AF on potentially dangerous offenders (PDOs). This addition alleviated the most common criticism of the AF, that it did not allow officers to record enough information about the offender. Three officers out of the five interviewed explicitly welcomed this *"chance to... record more information"* and another commented that *"with the framework you're giving a short picture of the situation but on the [additional forms] you're giving more thorough detail"*. One of these officers commented that: *"When there is risk of harm, I want to say specifically who against. ... I want to talk more about it and I want to have it more on the record than we've got space for here [in the AF]. ... And hopefully in my [Part] C that reflects that because I still do it there and I think anybody would with somebody who's dangerous."* Another officer said the combined AF and additional forms were useful when taking over a case in identifying the level of dangerousness.

One officer praised its utility in keeping them on track: *"it just helps to focus on, no matter what you're actually achieving, it sort of reminds you to, you know, what are you doing to sort of reduce the risk of harm."* Another officer said it was useful in formulating assessments: *"it's easy to say in one's opinion that a person is dangerous but you've got the three headings, antecedents, behaviour and conditions which one can't always keep in one's brain. It's a trigger, an excellent trigger."* The same officer also found the AF useful in managing risk of dangerous behaviour: *"it's also you know... an additional document to show the offender the risk has lessened to the extent that they've been taken, removed from the list. So instead of being classed as circling 'yes, they do present us a danger', one suddenly circles 'no' and one's able to prove that to the person and the reasons for it."* Two officers said it made assessments more concise and specific. Four of the officers said that overall they found the AF harm assessment "fairly useful".

8   Discussion and conclusions

This chapter draws together the findings of the study and discusses their implication for the implementation of any new national structured assessment of risk of re-offending and criminogenic needs.

Stand-alone v system

Four different models have been examined in the present study. The LSI-R is a stand-alone structured assessment form, which can theoretically be administered at any stage with an offender. (Additional supervision plans to fit in with the LSI-R are currently being designed.) ACE by contrast is a system, a series of forms, including an initial structured assessment form (which can be repeatedly administered), but also supervision plans and review forms. The Kent and Berkshire instruments, although single forms, are closer to systems than stand-alone assessments. The Kent CMI combines risk and needs assessments with case management. The Berkshire AF does not directly seek to structure the assessment of offenders, but asks officers to specify what outcomes are required to reduce the likelihood of re-offending over the life of an order, and incorporates reviews of these.

Figure 8.1 shows one model of the assessment supervision process. LSI-R provided only standardisation for the structured assessment itself. At the other end of the spectrum, ACE provided standardised schedules for all elements of the process, apart from the PSR. The Kent CMI structured the assessment and the reviews.

Figure 8.1 Interaction between different elements of assessment and supervision

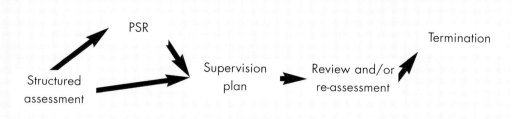

There are obvious trade-offs between implementing stand-alone assessments and systems:

- One of the strengths of the "systems", ACE, CMI and AF, was seen to be helping officers with supervision planning and with the supervision process in general, i.e. they fed directly into existing processes. Most ACE and CMI users said the initial assessments fed into the PSRs and supervision plans, but only half the LSI-R users said this was the case. By contrast, a more common criticism of LSI-R was that it did not help officers decide what to do with offenders.

- The most common criticism of ACE was that it was burdensome to complete. In particular, officers complained that it added to paperwork and there were too many forms within the system. This was not seen as so much of a problem for the other instruments (including the "single form" systems).

- Interestingly, three services using LSI-R had made moves to make the assessment less "stand-alone", by linking the final scores directly to the level of supervision that offenders received. One of these had also customised their preliminary supervision plan to fit in more closely with the LSI-R assessment. All of these services had constructed slightly different models of linkage. Thus, while assessments had possibly been made more consistent, the link between assessment and supervision was not necessarily so.

On balance, it would seem to be more profitable to put a system in place (whether this be based on the models of the existing systems looked at, or newly constructed around a stand-alone assessment), to ensure a smooth flow between the different elements of assessment and supervision, namely:

- structured assessments and PSRs/proposals for sentence;

- structured assessments/PSRs and supervision plans (see also the section: *Making links between assessed risk of re-offending and level of supervision*, below);

- supervision plans and the supervision process.

The minimal components of the system should comprise:

- an initial assessment;

- review forms for progress (not necessarily full re-assessments).

Optional extras might include:

- the PSR;

- the supervision plan;

- (full) re-assessments;

- self-assessments for offenders (see the section: *Including a tool for working directly with offenders*, below);

- termination forms (which might include re-assessment).

Some attempt should be made to tackle the main complaint against the biggest system, ACE - that of too much paperwork. There needs to be an examination of the necessity of all the forms (see also the section: *Reducing paperwork*, below). All forms within any new assessment system should be designed to link in with each other, otherwise time is wasted re-assimilating information to complete different paperwork. Concept and design points such as consistent layout, use of similar terminology and repetition of key phrases help to smooth transition between forms.

The new assessment procedure should be based on the "system" approach, linked into existing probation supervision procedures. The "system" should comprise, at minimum, an initial assessment, the supervision plan and review forms for progress.

When should the initial assessment be done?

There was some debate about when the initial assessment should be carried out. The majority of services in the study carried out the initial assessment at the PSR stage. However, one (West Midlands) did this post-PSR and officers using the Berkshire AF also sometimes did their initial assessment at the start of supervision. Briefly, the arguments for carrying out an assessment at PSR stage were:

- it would be available on those sentenced to custody and subsequently going on to probation supervision on license;

- the assessment would be available to feed into the PSR and proposals for sentence;

- although it was not brought up by officers, it can also be argued that the PSR stage represents the most critical point for an offender, when the decision about whether to send him or her to custody will be made, and therefore the fullest possible assessment should be available.

The arguments for carrying out the assessment post-PSR were:

- there was more time to do the assessment and form a working relationship with the offender;

- pre-sentence motivations made offenders more likely to conceal certain problems, or to agree to activities they had no intention of doing;

- there was no point carrying out a lengthy assessment on an offender when they were not going immediately onto probation supervision.

As the express aim of any new system will be to bring a common assessment for both the prison and probation service, the over-riding factor here is the need to provide consistent assessments on offenders whether they receive a community sentence or custody. The best way to achieve this consistency is to have assessments carried out of all offenders at the PSR stage, regardless of their sentence. (There is an issue here with offenders receiving neither a community sentence nor a prison sentence, for example, a fine or discharge: see the section: *Making links between identified needs and specified activities*, below.)

The arguments against doing initial assessments at the PSR stage therefore need to be tackled:

- About half the users of instruments said that assessments now took more time. This has implications for the workload of PSR writers. There is no point introducing structured, possibly lengthier assessments if there is not enough time to do them properly.

- There is a limit to how much pre-sentence motivations of offenders can be tackled, although this is a problem that any PSR writer would face, whether they had instruments or not. However, the new assessment system must give scope for assessments to be amended post-PSR. This should be kept to the minimum (if not optional), as in many cases very little time will elapse between the PSR and the start of an order, and no new circumstances will have arisen or come to light. For example, one LSI-R service filled in a one-page review form at the beginning of supervision, and the ACE system included an amendment form to be filled in at the start of supervision. (Subsequent changes would be picked up under the normal review procedures.)

- Another solution (not suggested by officers) which could in theory tackle both problems above is to have a more condensed PSR assessment and a fuller one at the start of supervision. However, it would be difficult to know what to omit from any condensed assessment, and this might be seen as repetitious.

- It must be made clear, either through training or guidance, that completing PSRs on offenders who subsequently go into custody may not be beneficial immediately, but will be in the longer-term, when these people come out on license. There were indications from officers supervising licenses that such pre-custodial assessments would be welcome and on occasion had already proved useful for them. It is usually more relevant for probation officers to have an indication of the offender's needs when they were last in the community, rather than a prison assessment of their needs in custody.

An initial assessment should be carried out at the PSR stage, for all offenders likely to go on to community supervision or custody. Provision should be made for amendments to the initial assessment subsequent to the start of supervision.

Design of the assessment/progress forms

The experiences of the ACE, LSI-R, CMI and AF users broadly reinforces the ground rules of form design:

- Items on the form must use clear and unambiguous wording. This was the main complaint that officers using ACE and LSI-R had when filling in the forms (see Chapter 4 for specific problems). Officers using LSI-R also had difficulty with jargon, double negatives and "American" language.

- The form itself needs to be self-explanatory. Fuller guidance should be given to officers, for example, in the form of a manual, but officers should not have to rely on the manual to fill in forms as a matter of course. The feeling about LSI-R, for instance, was that the form was slightly too brief for officers to be clear about the meaning of particular items.

- Subjectivity of questions and in particular coding was a problem for ACE users. This caused problems, for example, in measuring progress and in cases transferred between officers. In many cases, coding frames could be simplified or condensed or clearer guidance (including examples) given. Middle management may also have a role in ensuring consistency, as they could give a broader perspective across the team.

- The areas covered by the instruments were broadly felt to be the right ones to focus on, although there was a feeling that LSI-R in particular could be expanded.

- All of the items must be relevant (and seen to be relevant) to the assessment of risk of re-offending and criminogenic needs. This was mainly an issue for LSI-R.

- There should be flexibility for officers to collect information on non-criminogenic needs which may have a bearing on how offenders respond to supervision. For example, ACE asks officers to rate how offending-related a range of needs are. Another strategy, used by Kent, would be to specify particular needs/problems as non-criminogenic.

- There needs to be space for notes at each item, to highlight particular circumstances or explain apparent anomalies. This is important if the system is to be used for case recording, but also would make the forms more transparent, ease transfer of cases between officers, give room for officers' opinions and gut feelings, make the document easier to share with the offender and overcome officers' anxieties that they are being asked to fit offenders into boxes.

- The form should take account of the possibility of information being unavailable or unreliable, particularly if this is going to feed into a final score, which will in turn suggest, for example, supervision. Some officers were unhappy about having to rely on offenders for information for certain items, without being able to indicate this.

- The layout of the forms needs to be as simple and concise as possible, given the need to be self-explanatory and to allow space for notes.

Use of the initial assessment forms

One of the main benefits of all the instruments was that they were seen as improving the assessments, and the principal ways that this happened were in acting as a checklist to assessments, focusing on relevant areas and giving structure to the interview. In carrying out the interview, most officers used the forms as a discussion guide, rather than administering forms question by question. However, some officers were still using the forms in the latter way. There was scattered evidence that this caused problems in:

- officers believing that they had to rely on the offender for all information, when this could be gathered from other sources (particularly for LSI-R);

- making the interview more stilted and impeding the relationship with the offender;

- difficulties with using language from the forms, when they had not been designed for working with offenders (e.g. mental health section on LSI-R).

Officers could be encouraged to use the forms as a topic guide rather than a questionnaire, either through training, or through the use of tailored discussion guides for the interview along the lines of the West Glamorgan "pen picture". It should also be made clear that other sources of information apart from the offender can also be used to fill in the assessments, particularly existing files.

In assessment, officers should be encouraged to use the forms as topic guides, rather than questionnaires, and treat the offender as the main, but not only, source of information.

Including a tool for working directly with offenders

Only the ACE system specifically included a form designed directly for use with offenders, and this was seen as a strength of the system by 13 officers. This form was intended for use alongside the officer's assessment of an offender, so that both informed the supervision plan. Just under half the officers who used the self-completion questionnaire said it could start off discussions with the offenders, particularly if the officer and offender had different ideas about the offender's problems. However, there was scope for improvement to the clarity of the wording and clearer guidance on its use with offenders with reading or writing difficulties. A small number of users of other instruments found the instruments helpful in working with offenders.

There is much potential in designing the system so that offenders can be engaged in some way in the assessment process, or in measuring progress on an order. This would also tackle a concern by a small number of LSI-R users that it did not allow the offender to give their own views. Engaging offenders could be done either by:

- designing the officers' assessment/progress forms in such a way that they can be shared with offenders. The supervision plan should already fit this criteria as it has to be agreed with offenders. This could also include, for example, including visual or pictoral representations of problems, progress etc (see, for example, the assessment wheel in ACE).

- designing a form for offenders to fill in, either by themselves or with the officer. Allowing flexibility in this would be most useful, as offenders with reading/writing difficulties have problems with doing self-completion forms.

It is important not to over-estimate offenders' interest in being engaged with the system. Generally, their reactions to the forms were not overly positive, but there was a general acceptance that they had to fill in certain forms (and obviously with some individuals, a lot of interest in the forms). Offenders cannot be compelled to complete such a form, but there should be a strong expectation that they do so, given the useful role it can play within an assessment system. Again, there should be discretion/over-ride allowed in some cases not to use forms with offenders.

National Standards dictate that the supervision plan must be shared and agreed with offenders. Involving offenders in assessment would be, at the very least, additional and, more usefully, a prelude to this stage.

The experience of designing some forms, or elements of forms, for work with offenders was generally positive. There is scope for inclusion of a similar element in the new assessment system.

Using the forms to measure progress

The present study came up with some evidence about the performance of existing tools in measuring progress over an order, although it should be remembered that many officers had not yet used them for this purpose. About half of those who had used ACE, LSI-R and the AF had found it useful in reviewing work and highlighting improvements or lack of progress. Just under half the ACE users said a strength of the system was its ability to measure progress. However, half the officers said there were problems with measuring progress:

- with ACE, because very often little had changed, it increased paperwork and it did not add very much to existing procedures. Some officers also mentioned problems with consistency affecting measurement of progress (see the section: *Using the forms to measure progress,* above).

- with LSI-R, because it did not tell you why things were not working and the tick box format did not demonstrate progress very well, particularly when it was slight;

- with AF, because it did not adequately reflect progress.

These problems raise some questions for the form of the assessment system in measuring progress.

- Firstly, when should reviews and re-assessments be completed? There was varied practice in the services in the study, and no conclusive evidence that officers thought any one way was best. The main model for ACE was three-monthly reviews (of objectives) with full re-assessments every six or nine months. One ACE service also had a summary form at termination. A couple of LSI-R services were putting six-monthly re-assessments into place. Half the ACE and LSI-R users agreed there should be some form of re-assessment during supervision, but there was no consensus on what the re-assessment period should be. However, many officers were not thinking about full quarterly re-assessments, but reviews of existing objectives (as per the ACE model). Five of the ACE users thought even quarterly reviews were too frequent.

- The situation where officers are re-assessing static factors should be avoided. In measuring progress, officers should be focusing on dynamic factors which they are able to affect.

- The restriction of tick box formats in demonstrating progress, particularly for small changes (for example: a reduction in heroin use but with an ongoing problem) could partly be overcome by greater space for details. While the focus will be on whether specified objectives have been achieved, there should be opportunity for officers to record any changes or progress, even if they do not alter or are not directly related to the objectives.

- Giving the assessment role a clear role in case management, so that methods, referrals and agencies involved in working with the offender are recorded, may help officers (and middle managers) to look at what methods are working, and why potential problems are occurring.

There was little discussion about any "disclosure effects" occurring, although about a quarter of LSI-R users said that when they disagreed with another officer's assessment, this was because the offender had revealed more. There was also the suggestion that offenders often revealed more problems after the PSR stage. Any system to monitor progress will need to take account of these effects, to avoid the situation where offenders' problems apparently "worsen" over the course of an order.

In designing forms to measure progress, the range of interested parties also needs to be borne in mind, that is:

- showing offenders how much or how little progress they have made, forms to share with offenders;

- allowing officers to look at progress over an order, in order to evaluate what is working and what is not - this also ties in with case management;

- providing information to middle management to assess progress on an order - both how the offender is doing and how the officer is using their time and resources available to them (including making referrals);

- giving information to service management about overall service performance, including input into what programmes/activities/partnerships are effective;

- demonstrating performance of the service as a whole, e.g. to the Home Office, HMIP inspectors, or the wider public.

In particular, forms designed to show offenders how much or little progress they have made may be very different to those used for fulfilling the needs of the other parties listed above.

The assessment system could potentially play an active role in measuring and demonstrating progress to officers, offenders and other interested parties. However, reviews and re-assessments need to be timed as parsimoniously as possible, and scope should be given for measuring both change towards specified objectives, and other changes which do not meet or fit those criteria.

Making links between assessed risk of re-offending and level of supervision

Three of the LSI-R services had made explicit links between the final LSI-R score and the level of supervision offenders received. One ACE service was also examining moves towards linking the ACE scores with supervision. The Kent CMI was also seen to have potential in determining when offenders were ready to go onto their reporting schemes (i.e. for lower risk offenders).

There is certainly scope for making more explicit links between levels of assessed risk (of re-offending) and levels or form of supervision. This would:

- recommend (not prescribe) levels of supervision or activities for offenders with certain levels of risk;

- encourage consistency between services in what they provide and how they deal with offenders;

- provide back-up to officers' decisions, for example, in cases where low-risk offenders are being recommended for a lighter sentence below the threshold of community penalties;

- take into account the different forms of probation supervision, namely probation orders, combination orders or community service orders.

However, any such structure would:

- need to be subject to over-ride by officers for individual cases;

---

8   Officers were not specifically asked to comment on the use of the assessment forms for offenders on community service orders (CSOs). Where assessments were completed at the PSR stage, use was not particularly dependent on the proposed sentence, so that assessments were completed for people recommended for CSOs. In one ACE area, offenders on CSOs had the initial assessment form completed, but no subsequent parts of the ACE system.

- allow for other criteria to be taken into account in deciding levels of supervision, primarily risk of harm;

- be based on meaningful bandings of risk, preferably established by research, to minimise the use of the over-ride and retain credibility with officers.

Guidance could be in the form of recommendation for minimum supervision frequency for certain levels of risk groups, and there might be scope for including a summary of links on the forms themselves. These links could be broad enough to take account of variation in local service provision (for example, very low risk would mean a minimum of once-a-week contact and referral to outside agencies).

Construction of a structure for making explicit links between levels of assessed risk of re-offending and levels or form of supervision should be explored in the new system.

Making links between identified needs and specific activities

(a) Triggering referrals

Another area which was touched on by some of the assessment systems was that of the presence of specific problems triggering specific actions to deal with them. Examples in the current study were:

- in one LSI-R service, identification of a drugs problem led to specific referral to a project;

- there were examples of more informal links being made by some officers, for example, between drugs and alcohol problems and referrals to specific projects;

- some CMI users cited a strength of the instrument being that it aided referral to outside agencies.

Development of this area could be streamlined with development of the case management aspects of some of the systems looked at, mainly CMI and ACE, in effect, making them a more proactive version of case management.

(b)   Triggering other assessments

In addition, the assessments were seen as unsuitable for certain sub-groups, primarily "dangerous" offenders, for example, sexual offenders. Other groups that some officers saw as unsuited to the main structured assessments were juveniles, women, and ethnic minorities. Simple expansion of the assessment instruments is not possible for all these different exceptions, as it would result in much lengthier assessments, and many offenders being asked irrelevant or inappropriate questions. The assessments were already seen by some officers as "overkill" for some motoring (particularly drunk drivers) and more trivial offenders.

Some LSI-R users were also unhappy with the mental health assessment, as they felt unqualified to make such judgements.

There may be therefore more scope for using the initial assessments, or reviews, as definite triggers for:

- specific assessments, possibly carried out by specialists other than probation officers. For example, it may be possible to simplify the LSI-R mental health assessment and instead use the form to trigger a specific assessment of this in case of concern.

- more detailed assessments to be carried out on particular groups, for example, domestic violence cases. In some cases, such as juveniles, it may be preferable to fill in alternative forms, but some groups can only be identified during assessment. In connection with this, the point was also made that sexual problems or domestic violence may still be an issue even if these are not the offences for which offenders are being tried.

Tackling officers' feelings that the assessments were too much for certain cases is more difficult. One solution to this would be to make the assessment more general, so that only very basic questions were asked. However, officers did not give any indications that they thought particular parts of the assessment were unnecessary so it is difficult to know what could be cut out, and in most cases would still need a fuller assessment. An alternative strategy would be to allow officers not to complete the risk assessment for certain groups, for example, where they do not envisage recommending a community penalty or custodial sentence. However, in these cases, they would have to carry out some form of assessment to determine this, so in the interests of consistency, this should be the same basic assessment as for all offenders. Drink-drivers emerged as one distinct group which officers said often did not have many problems or needs that they could work with. This suggests that there may be scope for using simplified or alternative assessments for such offenders, but it also raises a wider question of how much work can be done with this group within probation, if there are no identified needs for officers to work with.

The feasibility of making the initial assessment act as a trigger for referrals and other assessments should be examined.

Should the new system include risk of harm?

There were various ways of assessing risk of harm found in the study, although no single way emerged as the "best" way to deal with it. Examples included:

- ACE risk of harm used as a reflection of other concurrent procedures (Hereford and Worcester) and as the main risk of harm assessment (e.g. West Midlands);

- LSI-R risk of re-offending and risk of harm procedures being separate and concurrent (e.g. Durham), with one service (Surrey) using LSI-R risk of re-offending as a potential route to a fuller risk of harm assessment;

- risk of harm being a separate procedure within one instrument (Kent and Berkshire) tools).

LSI-R was not designed to cover risk of harm. However, about half its users felt that it could and should be expanded to include this. At the other end of the spectrum, all the Kent and Berkshire users found the incorporated risk of harm assessment useful. The evidence from ACE was fairly ambiguous: it was used both as a summary of other risk of harm assessments, and as one in its own right. About half the ACE users said they found it useful, but there was no indication that it was more or less useful as a summary or assessment proper.

Possible reasons for incorporating a full risk of harm assessment into a new system can be summarised as:

- it does not seem to lead to confusion between the two concepts, and the format of assessments could be kept distinct.

- there are several models for risk of harm assessments which it would be feasible to incorporate into the new system, for example, the Kent and Berkshire checklists, the Brearley model. (A purely "tick-box" approach would probably not be suitable.)

- the assessments tend to be parallel in nature, that is, they need to be assessed and reviewed at similar times, and are often required at similar stages, for example, to feed into supervision planning. They also occasionally overlap (some of the same factors considered). It therefore makes sense to draw them together.

- risk of re-offending and risk of harm in the same document would highlight and provide a fuller picture of those individuals where the two risks are not the same (given that officers had concerns when apparently "dangerous" individuals had a low assessed risk of re-offending).

- there may be a psychological advantage in "cutting down on paperwork".

Alternative measures might be:

- to include summary measures of concurrent risk of harm procedures, to flag up high risk of harm offenders and provide a fuller picture of individuals. This would involve some duplication of form-filling by officers.

- some services (not necessarily included in the study) carry out less detailed risk of harm assessments on all offenders, which serve to flag up dangerous offenders for a fuller assessment. The new system could incorporate this stage of risk of harm assessment only.

The scope for including risk of harm needs to be examined further. Possible models for incorporation exist.

The new system and case management

All the systems looked at incorporated a case management role to a greater or lesser extent, although officers were not asked to comment on its role in this. The models in the study were:

- the Kent CMI uses codes to indicate which agency was tackling which identified need. Users said the instrument helped them in case management, aided referral out to programmes and other resources and gave structure to supervision.

- the ACE supervision plans and review forms include codes to specify which methods will be used to tackle objectives.

- some of the Berkshire AF outcome codes referred to particular programmes.

There is definite scope for the instrument to feed into case management, including provision of information on work done and resources used. This could be developed in conjunction with more specific links between assessments and specific activities.

The new system and case recording

None of the instruments examined performed the role of case recording particularly satisfactorily. The majority of users of the more condensed forms (LSI-R and AF) said they were not useful for this, as did half the CMI users. Even ACE, which has more space for notes and evidence, did not do very well on this aspect: six officers said it was not useful (compared to eight who said it was). All of the instruments were also criticised because of the limitations in the forms in some respects: LSI-R because it did not give enough scope for officer opinions; ACE and CMI because they did not always give a true picture of offenders, and the AF because it was not felt to be very transparent. Fewer officers said provision of information was a strength of the forms, although AF and to a lesser extent LSI-R were felt to provide a good summary for officers.

The role of the system in case recording needs to be clarified. One alternative would be to make it clear that the new system is **not** about case recording. In which case, its role as a summary of a case should be strengthened, and the forms themselves made concise rather than lengthy. However, more officers complained about condensed forms than welcomed their use as a summary.

This would then suggest the other alternative, i.e. to design the forms with their role as case record in mind. They would then need to be able to record the progress of the order, rather than just outcomes, and reasons for success/failure, alternative strategies tried, contacts made and so on. The role of supplementary notes would become important, if not compulsory.

The system should aim to be a case record for the officer. It should therefore be designed to record the progress of the order, with space for notes.

Reducing paperwork

From the practitioners' perspective, a major issue is reducing or streamlining paperwork. The added paperwork of the forms was particularly mentioned by ACE users, and to a lesser extent by LSI-R and CMI users. There was also felt to be overlap with risk of harm forms and repetition of standard information, such as, demographics and monitoring forms. This could be reduced by one or more of the following strategies (some of which are mentioned elsewhere where they are relevant):

- linking the roll-out of any system closely to CRAMS and ideally giving a computerised version which is compatible with CRAMS. This version should allow data to be entered easily onto the system, make use of existing information and allowing information to be pulled off the system at individual-, officer- and team-level. Standard information about the offender, for example, age, sex, offence, should only need to be entered once for each case.

- ensuring that any national roll-out replaces other forms or reduces overlap as necessary, for example, monitoring forms;

- drawing risk of harm and risk of re-offending assessments together;

- making prison and probation risk assessments more compatible;

- being parsimonious about the length and number of forms in the systems;

- reducing the length of forms for general offenders and only triggering more specialised assessments for certain groups;

- keeping the frequency of reviews or re-assessments to a minimum.

The introduction of the new assessment system should be linked as closely as possible to CRAMS and/or computerisation, and align with existing systems as far as possible. The assessment system itself should keep form-filling to the minimum required.

Linking prison and probation assessments

This was not a specific concern of the study, but some officers commented on the difficulties caused by inconsistencies between the systems, within the prison system itself, and duplication of the systems. Generally, moves to bring the systems closer together would be welcomed, although no details were collected about how this could be done. However, any moves to bring the risk of re-offending assessments together need to be co-ordinated with risk of harm and dangerousness assessments. In addition, some attention should be paid to other agencies carrying out risk assessments, for example, health and social services and the Police.

Standardisation vs flexibility

There is a general tension between standardising the instrument to encourage consistency between officers and ultimately services, to allow effectiveness to be measured and in practical terms for it to be evidence-based; and allowing some flexibility to take account of potential differences between services in terms of caseload (e.g. a rural area vs an inner city) and to allow the instrument to develop and for valid concerns or problems to be tackled.

Some strategies for allowing flexibility within a fixed structure would be:

- specify a core assessment structure but allow services to add some extra items (as ACE does currently).

- allow for say yearly/two-yearly revisions of the instrument to incorporate developments and improvements.

- set up local/national groups of practitioners to feed comments in to revised versions of the instrument. These groups could also suggest local additions to the instrument.

- allow local research/evaluation to feed into development of the instrument at a local level.

Training and guidance

Some officers spoke about the introduction of the new instruments into the service. There was mention of initial resistance to the instruments, although motivations for this were unclear. Possible reasons given were: lack of training, reluctance to change, limitations of the instruments to work (e.g. sex offenders), seeing instruments as not adding much to probation officers' work or skills, and increased paperwork. It may be worth asking those services who have already introduced instruments about their experiences with officers' acceptance of the instrument. However, some tentative lessons can be suggested from the research, particularly about the form and design of the initial training:

- The training for any new risk/needs assessment system should not be seen separately from ongoing evaluation and development of the new system. It is important that there is an active practitioner input into the development of the form, to ensure that problems with implementation are tackled before the introduction of the new system, and to instill a feeling of ownership. Practitioner input into draft versions of the new instrument could be encouraged, through piloting draft versions, via practitioner advisory groups to the development of the form or through feedback from consultations with services and officers.

- The initial training should clearly explain the purpose of the instrument. Officers gave varied responses to this question.

- There should be some brief explanation of the theories underlying the instrument, although there is no need to go into great amounts of detail. (For example, a video used in the LSI-R training was generally not well received.)

- It should clearly justify the inclusion of each item, or in certain cases, the omission of certain items.

- The training should be hands-on, with plenty of examples and practical exercises. It must relate to work within the probation service.

- It should set out the best way to administer the instruments, encouraging a "topic guide" approach rather than having forms used as a questionnaire, and emphasising that forms can also be completed from other information available, not just offenders.

- The potential benefits of the instruments should be made clear. That is, it can improve assessments and supervision planning, be used to work directly with offenders and provide credibility to officers' assessments, both as back-up to their own feelings and to other parties such as the courts.

- Trainers should also be open about the limitations of the instrument, including the limitations imposed by any form.

- The delivery of the training should be tailored to the different needs and expectations that new and more experienced officers might have. Newer officers may find the instruments useful as a checklist for assessments and structure for working. However, long-serving officers are unlikely to find them as beneficial in this. Indeed, it was often commented that the new instruments should not make a lot of difference to good officers' practice. The benefits for more experienced officers may come more from issues of consistency, credibility and accountability. The fact is that for some officers, the instruments will not affect their practice much, and this should be stressed.

- The training must focus on and answer officers' queries and concerns and allow for some feedback on the system. (However, officers' expectation should not be raised unduly, as the instrument will not be amenable to immediate change.) Involving other users in giving the training may be useful in this respect.

- The training for any new assessment system should link in with What Works training and other initiatives, such as CRAMS.

- One device which was well received was to split the training to allow officers to use the instrument in practice and then come back to more training, so they can raise particular concerns and issues that have arisen in practice.

- Training on the new instrument must be part of any induction programme, so that new officers do not begin work untrained in the new instrument. Two officers in the ACE sample who had been in this position had not received any formal training, and felt the lack of it.

Appendix A: List Of Questions Asked In Interviews

The following questions were used as a guide to interviews in each of the areas. Some slight adjustments were made to the questionnaire after interviewing in the first service (Northumbria). Unless indicated, the same questions were asked of ACE, LSI-R, CMI and AF users.

Probation officers

How long have you worked in probation? How long have you worked in this service area? Specific duties involved in current job.
Is your use of {instrument} current/in the past?
When did you start using {instrument}? For past use: when did you stop using it?

How much training did you have for {instrument}?
Who provided it?
Was the amount of training suitable? If no: how could it have been improved?
Was the content of the training suitable? If no: how could it have been improved?

What do you see as the main purpose of {instrument}?
At what stages do you normally complete {instrument}? For each stage, ask: approximately how long do you spend filling out the form(s) at this stage?
ACE users only asked for Initial assessment form, Self completion, Supervision plan, Quarterly progress forms, Other: Which parts of the form do you use: always, often, occasionally, never?
ACE, LSI-R and CMI users only: Is it clear to you how to interpret the scores? Why is that?

If completed at PSR stage:
How does {instrument} contribute to the PSR and proposals for sentence?
How useful do you find {instrument} at the PSR stage? Why do you say that?

If completed at the start of supervision:
How does {instrument} contribute to supervision planning for an offender?
How useful do you think {instrument} is for drawing up supervision plans or for specifying activities or treatment? Why do you say that?

If completed during supervision:

How do these (re)assessments affect the offender's subsequent supervision or activities?

What would you say was the main aim of assessment at this stage?

How useful do you think {instrument} is for measuring an offender's progress on an order? Why do you say that?

Do assessments using {instruments} take more or less time than assessments of offenders made without them? If more/less: how much more/less time does {instrument} take? Why is that?

In general, do you use the form as a general guide to discussion or fill it in with the offender question by question?

Is the offender involved in completing the form? How much? How do clients react to you using {instrument}?

Do you find that the assessment form legitimised asking offenders certain questions? Which questions and why do you think this was?

When you took over a case where someone else had carried out an assessment, did you usually find you broadly agreed with their assessment {for Berkshire: outcomes specified}? If no, why do you think this was?

Have you had any access to {instrument} in a computerised form? If yes, how useful have you found this?

Has using {instrument} made any difference to the way you work? If yes, what kinds of differences? If no, why do you say that?

Do you think {instrument; ACE version read "ACE and OGRS"} asks the right questions about offenders in terms of measuring risks (of re-offending)? If no, why do you say that? {Berkshire version asked: do you think the outcomes listed in the assessment framework are the right ones in terms of reducing risks of re-offending?}

Do you think {instrument} asks the right questions about offenders in terms of measuring needs? If no, why do you say that? {Berkshire version asked: do you think the assessment framework outcomes are the right ones to cover offenders' needs?}

Does {instrument} have categories or provide scales which are generally appropriate for your clients? If no, why do you say that? {Berkshire version asked: do you find it easy to fit people into the different outcomes?

To what extent do you feel there is an overlap between the information you have to enter for {instrument} and that on other forms which you complete?

Are there any questions or parts of {instrument} that you think are unnecessary? If yes, which parts/questions?

Do you think {instrument} misses out any factors {Berkshire: outcomes} which are important in measuring risks or needs? If yes, which ones?

How useful do you think {instrument; ACE version read OGRS} is for predicting risk of reconviction? Why do you say that? {Berkshire version asked: how useful do you think the assessment framework is for reducing the likelihood of offending?}

How useful do you think {instrument} is for helping you to prioritise problems to be addressed? Why do you say that?

How useful do you think {instrument} is for recording information about a case? Why do you say that?

ACE, CMI, AF users only: How useful do you find the {instrument} risk of harm assessment? Why do you say that?

Overall, how useful have you found {instrument} in your work with offenders? Why do you say that?

Have you found any other benefits in using {instrument}? If yes, what sort of benefits?

Have you experienced any problems in using {instrument}?

Do you think {instrument} is suitable for all the types of client you deal with? If no, who is it unsuitable for? Why do you say that? What methods or approaches are suitable for assessing risk for this group? What methods or approaches are suitable for assessing their needs?

When do you think are the best times to complete {instrument}? Why do you think that?

Do you think {instrument} could be improved in any way? If yes, how?

Overall, would you say {instrument} is a good or bad thing? (Note: this was dropped from later interviews, as the question was overly repetitive.)

LSI-R users only: What procedures are currently in place for you to measure risk of harm? Do you think LSI-R contributes to risk of harm assessments in any way? If yes, how?

In addition to {instrument}, do you now or have you in the past used any other types of tools which assess risks or needs? This could include specialist tools designed for specific types of offenders and assessments to measure risk of harm or dangerousness. If yes, which ones? Which groups of offenders is it used for? How useful have you found these tools? Do you think they add anything to assessments made by {instrument}? If yes, what do they add? Would you recommend that the probation service used {instrument in the future or not}?

Senior Probation Officers

How long have you worked in probation? How long have you worked in this service area? Specific duties involved in current job.
Is your team's use of {instrument} current/in the past?
When did you start using {instrument}? For past use: when did you stop using it?
Do all members of staff that you manage use {instrument} or only some of them? If only some, why is that?
Do you yourself use {instrument} to make assessments of offenders or for PSRs? Have you used {instrument} in the past?

What do you see as the main purpose of {instrument}?
At what stages do your officers normally complete {instrument}?
Have you observed any changes in your staff's performance as a result of using {instrument}? If yes, what sort of changes?

Has the introduction of {instrument} made any difference to the way you work? If yes, what kind of differences? If no, why not?
In general, is the use of {instrument} discussed in team meetings? If yes, what sort of issues come up?

If team completes at PSR stage:
How useful do you think {instrument} is at the PSR stage? Why do you say that?

If team completes at the start of supervision:
How useful do you think {instrument} is for supervision planning? Why do you say that?

If team completes during supervision:
How useful do you think {instrument} is for measuring an offender's progress? Why do you say that?
How useful do you think {instrument} is for ensuring consistency of assessments between officers? Why do you say that?
How useful do you think {instrument} is for quality control of assessment procedures? Why do you say that?
How useful do you think {instrument} is for quality control of supervision procedures or activities? Why do you say that?
How useful do you think {instrument} is for controlling other aspects of staff's performance? Why do you say that?

How useful do you think {instrument} is for managing staff caseloads? Why do you say that?
How useful do you think {instrument} is for general management information purposes? Why do you say that?

Do you think there are any other benefits in using {instrument}? If yes, what sort of benefits?
Have there been any problems in using {instruments}?
Do you think {instrument} could be improved in any way? If yes, how?
Do you use {instrument} to directly refer offenders to particular programmes? If yes, which programmes are these and what are the criteria for reference?

Overall, would you say {instrument} is a good or bad thing? (Note: this was dropped from later interviews, as the question was overly repetitive.)
In addition to {instrument}, does your team use any other types of tools which assess risks or needs? This could include specialist tools designed for specific types of offenders and assessments to measure risk of harm or dangerousness. Have they in the past? If yes, which ones? Which groups of offenders is it used for? How useful have you found these tools? Do you think they add anything to assessments made by {instrument}? If yes, what do they add? Would you recommend that the probation service used {instrument in the future or not}?

Aubrey,R. and Hough,M. (1997) *Assessing Offendersí Needs: Assessment Scales for the Probation Service*. Home Office Research Study No 166. London: Home Office.

Brearley, C.P. (1982). *Risk and Social Work: Hazards and Helping*. London, Routledge and Kegan Paul.

Burnett, R. (1996). *Fitting Supervision to Offenders: assessment and allocation decisions in the Probation Service*. Home Office Research Study No 153. London: Home Office.

Chapman, T. and Hough, M. (1998). *Evidence Based Practice: a guide to effective practice*. Edited by M. Jane Furniss. London: HM Inspectorate of Probation.

Copas, J.B. (1998). *The Offending Group Reconviction Scale: a statistical reconviction score for use by Probation Officers*. Applied Statistics, Volume 47, Part 1.

HMI Probation (1995). *Dealing with Dangerous People: the probation service and public protection*. Report of a Thematic Inspection. London: Home Office.

Kemshall, H. (1996). *Reviewing Risk: A Review of Research on the Assessment and Management of Risk and Dangerousness: implications for policy and practice in the Probation Service*. London: Home Office.

RDS Publications

Requests for Publications

Copies of our publications and a list of those currently available may be obtained from:

Home Office
Research, Development and Statistics Directorate
Communications Development Unit
Room 201, Home Office
50 Queen Anne's Gate
London SW1H 9AT
Telephone: 020 7273 2084 (answerphone outside of office hours)
Facsimile: 020 7222 0211
E-mail: publications.rds@homeoffice.gsi.gov.uk

alternatively

why not visit the RDS web-site at
Internet: http://www.homeoffice.gov.uk/rds/index.htm

where many of our publications are available to be read on screen or downloaded for printing.